The Art of Shallow Neighboring

BUILDING SHALLOW RELATIONSHIPS WITH YOUR EIGHT CLOSEST NEIGHBORS

THOMAS MUROSKY, PH.D.

Our Walk In Christ Publishing
State College, PA

Published by Our Walk in Christ
www.ourwalkinchrist.com

The Art of Shallow Neighboring: Building Shallow Relationships with Your Eight Closest Neighbors

First Printing 2017
ISBN-13: 978-1976226519
ISBN-10: 1976226511

The stories in this book are fictional parodies of the source material.

The Internet addresses, email addresses, and phone numbers in this book are accurate at the time of publication. They are provided as a resource, but due to the nature of the Internet, those addresses may change.

To Christians everywhere tired of business practices
and buzz words infiltrating the church.

Contents

Acknowledgments

Many people whom I know laughed like hysterical hyenas when I said I was going to dribble some words on paper and call it a 'book', but others encouraged me to write something so shallow the morning sun would vanquish the roots of seed sown into sandy soil. I wish to acknowledge the latter people and say to the former, "neener, neener, neener, I wrote a Bo-ook!"

Firstly, I am grateful to the consortium of pastors, most of whom I intentionally chose *not* to sit under their shallow teaching, for their attempt to become the Holy Spirit in my life. Without their effort to define my ministry, I would not have known the power of Block Parties of Salvation. You, though nameless, have been a significant part of this story.

I would also like to acknowledge the local business community. Thanks to the regular adult beverage consumption in the business meetings in our town, many people now feel an emptiness leading them to prescription drug abuse in our quaint metropolis. As a result, pastors started to look for how to help the community, which led to an amazing church movement. Without their dedication to a pragmatic model that worked 1500 miles away by a mayor who funds block parties, we would have never thought about Block Parties of Salvation locally. We also thank you that you could clarify the mission of the local pastors because the Bible is no longer relevant in guiding the local church.

A number of people have served as my mentors and friends while I sat in a fetal position induced by over-consumption of the evening news. During this time when I was afraid to talk to my neighbors, you have been the ones to lend me a supporting hand. Thank you for leaning in and making me intentional to love Jesus so I felt connected enough to approach my neighbors with my missional task of throwing a Block Party of Salvation.

I also wish to thank my editor. I did not have the nerve to find someone locally because that might mean knocking on some doors, but anyway, a very special thanks to the Scots-Irish crazy lady who said her name was 'Kate', but hey, it was on the Internet, so I know it is true.

I would thank my agent, but all those I approached with the idea of writing a book about having a block party in order to save souls all opened their eyes wide and slowly backed away from me toward the door. I think they were concerned I would make them save all their neighbors the way I was going to save mine.

1

Oh, That's My Neighbor

What if we all just opened our dusty Bibles we have been speaking so highly of for two thousand years to find that living by it's principles would actually help us solve societies problems? We might even read that Jesus said the greatest commandment was to "Love the Lord your God with all your heart, all your soul, all your mind, and all your strength." We might even read that the *second* of those commands is to love your neighbor as yourself. I know what you are thinking...who is my neighbor? Don't worry! We will not talk about that in our chapter on defining your neighbor. Rather than letting the Bible inform our definition of a neighbor (because that would run contrary to our present scheme), we will use anecdotal stories to make your emotions define your neighbor for you!

I know, we should all love our neighbors so much that when God said his word should be on our hearts, tied to our hands, bound on our foreheads, and written on our doorposts (Deuteronomy 6:4-9) our consumer-focused nature brought us to buy Jesus Junk with all manner of Bible verses and Christian slogans in the form of T-Shirts, bumper stickers, bracelets, and tattoos. We proudly wear these 'proofs' that we are saved because it is virtually impossible to discern we have made any commitment to Jesus by the way we live our lives. Come on, if we were really saved, we would know the names, goals, and dreams of the people in the eight closest houses to ours on the block.

I know what you are all thinking. Considering the terrifying news that we choose to consume every day, going to visit the neighbors is like dropping off gifts to the Auca Indians! Those savages might be flinging children across the room while guzzling power-funnels of pure moonshine. The strange teenage girl over there might be pregnant, and if not, that teenage boy has surely cast his seed across the town causing the next birthing bubble! Truly, the savages on my block would fry me up like Hannibal Lecter! Considering they can't mow their lawns, the teenagers might be smoking some weed while they play Battlefield, and with all these foreigners who speak other languages I just feel overwhelmed! I know, we should just call the National Guard!

But what if the neighbors are not the savages we have convinced ourselves that they are? What if we got to know the people on the block and they were not blood-thirsty Auca Indians? What if they are just longing for someone to throw a block party so the whole neighborhood would just start holding hands and spontaneously while singing 'Imagine'? What if they all just wanted to be something some day, but can't act until a hero organizes a block party that will surely nudge them into their dreams? What truly would happen if you created that Block Party of Salvation with the final goal of telling everyone on your block about the shallow relationship you have with Jesus?

Finally a Messenger We Can Hear

We all know the horrible social problems facing America, in fact we fear them, because we choose to become couch-bound vegetables fixing our eyes devotionally to our television sets night after night. We see the images of the at-risk kids selling drugs in poverty stricken areas full of dilapidated housing. Children are hungry in the streets because the food stamps are being hocked for liquor and drugs. People are lonely and the elderly have become shut-ins whom society has forgotten to check up on. We could drone on about this for hours but since we all sit transfixed to endless and mindless television, we all get the point: Our neighborhoods are falling into ruin!

I joined a group of pastors from around town and we searched and searched our Bibles for about a minute and could not find anywhere God gave us a three-point plan to solve the problems highlighted on our television sets, so we invited the local mayor to ask him what we should do. It was shocking! The Mayor spewed forth four powerful letters: W-W-J-D. That is right, he prodded us to live just like Jesus commanded us by being good to our literal neighbors! Now we had a plan! We knew we needed to search the Bible for verses we could twist to fit into the narrative we wanted to push: That Jesus was really only talking about saving the people in the eight houses closest to us on our block. Once everyone helps those in the eight closest houses on the block, the elderly shut-ins will be visited by the person in the next house, and fatherless children will be mentored by that strange single man down the street!

We left the meeting totally shocked that all our Seminary study failed us in leading our congregants to be good neighbors, but the local Mayor gave us all the insight we needed! We were embarrassed. We knew all about the late night news and the trendy television programs so we could connect with the desperate souls our congregants dragged to church, but we did not realize that obeying Jesus would help us solve the problems in our very city. We all collectively looked around the room like a cow staring at a new gate before arriving at the shocking final thought: One of us remembered vaguely that a verse in the Bible said something about a neighbor, so we consulted Google and found Matthew 22:37-40 which says:

Jesus replied: "'Love the Lord your God with all your heart and with all your soul and with all your mind.' this is the first and greatest commandment. And the second is like it: 'Love your neighbor as yourself.' All the Law and the Prophets hang on these two commandments."

But we encountered an automatic interpretive challenge that Jesus delineates between a first and a second commandment, but we do not want to deal with what it means to love the Lord your God with all your heart, so we chose instead to write the verse number but write that Jesus combined those together so we could now define a new proper noun throughout the rest of this book: Great Commandment. This allows us to talk about a Great Commandment without dealing with that pesky 'loving God' part and make it sound like the first commandment is really to love your neighbor!

It came across all our collective minds, that this Jesus guy truly was a great moral teacher! He must be a genius, the only other way he could know all this stuff was if he was a god or something!

On our next meeting we wanted to seek the advice from other city officials, so we invited someone frustrated that 'Christians' are not living like Christians, and that forged us into a steel, rigid structure and we knew the only thing we could do was establish a three-point program to save people through community block parties. We had this final meeting and decided it was time to start a full sermon series consisting of buzz words like kingdom-minded, kingdom-focus, connected, lean in, intentional, and more just to make it sound all hip and worldly. That is exactly what it takes to bring a missionally-focused church to the next level so we can all start throwing our own Block Parties of Salvation.

First Step to Saving the Block

If you are buying this junk like I am, than your head is probably spinning in circles like that girl on *The Exorcist* because your schedule is so full of television you do not have the time to throw a Block Party of Salvation. Regardless, I think you should lean-in to the idea that Jesus was a genius who commanded us to throw block parties, so failing to drop everything to learn the names and aspirations of the eight closest people to you might mean you forfeit your place in heaven. You don't want to burn in hell, do you, do you?!

The first step is to take the commandments of Jesus literally and seriously. I have seen too many Christian slogans come and go in my day, and this book will be no different, but we will use different slogans because it is clear the slogans we have been using do not work. I know the solution to society's problems is not found in government programs and church attendance. People will only begin to get their needs met when every block starts throwing their own party, so take that fish symbol off your car and replace it with our tic-tac-toe grid to show everyone that you know the aspirations of the people living in the eight closest houses to you.

An Epiphany on Neighboring

When I first left teaching to become a pastor, I went from speaking to thirty people to audiences over a thousand in number! I only say this so you will be impressed at my audience numbers. It is also of importance that I became the pastor of a church that was so shallow people only used it as a dating service. That is only relevant because it means lots of people showed up on Sunday morning including pastors and other church leaders who coveted adding bodies to the church building and wanted to know what we were doing to grow so fast. Speaking at this church often times meant I felt lonely going home at night like a rock star after his concert. I was totally empty because Jesus was just a slogan to me, but other people were not buying my slogan because they were just not reorganizing their life around my pastoral rock concert. I realized that large churches do not help people to transform their life because children were still being drug dealers in old dilapidated buildings. Our single church could not save our city no matter how many people we draw in with Christian entertainment. It was also clear that God was not doing it, so we needed to consult some business people to find out what they said to do.

I eventually left that church because child drug dealers were not being saved, and I found a new church that was also growing like a tomato on Miracle Grow®. During this time I was reading John 17 a lot, but I don't want to bore anyone or bother this book's marketing team with long, clear exposition, and of course, I want to bank on most people not reading what I am talking about because I want to twist it around to make my point. Anyway, Jesus is on total fire for all of us to be in perfect unity like one of those seventies communes, but more importantly, that our oneness will draw other people to God. I know that is not what John 17:23 says, but like I said, I am banking on people not verifying what I preach. Regardless, this epiphany caused us to drop our Bibles and flock to hear the local mayor define God's mission for all our congregations in the city, this led me to the final conclusion of the matter: Jesus was really talking about my literal neighbor, not whomever I might encounter in need as I live my life.

The Way to Save the Block

Once again I want to reiterate that Jesus was really smart! He told us to ignore the whole, huge, burdensome Bible full of scary sounding words and only do two things: Love God and love your neighbor. I mean, really, if you think about it, that is only one thing we all need to do! If you just follow the road map to this one command, you, too, will finally find the peace you have been looking for, and more importantly, you will become the person whom God has declared forever that you shall become! After all, if you are not a neighbor to the people living in the eight closest houses to you, you will not experience the good life Jesus promised you!

2

Seriously Twisting the Greatest Commandment

A few years ago I worked in a church that was busting at the seams with new people whom did not know what it meant to be a Christian but they warmed our chairs on Sunday morning so all was well. My job was to borrow entertainment activities from the culture so people would invite their friends to be baited-and-switched into hearing a message about loving Jesus so we could make our shallow wading pool of a church wider by leaps and bounds. After all, saying a little prayer about Jesus will bring about good fortune in our lives, and bonus! We will not have to burn in hell for all the fun stuff we like to do!

Anyway, I planned some worldly concert with a famous band...something like Mr. Manson or something like that, I don't know, I just booked who was popular at that time. We had lasers and a smoke machine to make it seem like the people were really there for the concert. Even though we planned for several thousand people, only a couple hundred showed even after I begged everyone in my Rolodex to bring two friends. I just knew I failed to expand the bounds of my wading pool so I was worried about my job. My church buddies accompanied me to a local bar so I could drown my sorrows but I was shocked to find all the people we wanted to strong-arm into praying for Jesus were here, so I asked the hostess why it was so busy. She yelled, 'What?", so I yelled back, "WHY IS IT SO BUSY IN HERE?", and she barked, "IT IS BECAUSE OF THIS CONCERT WE ARE HAVING...CAN'T YOU HEAR THEM?"

Suddenly it hit me like a ton of bricks! We realized that most people were not duped by our pretend concert in the church so they all came here instead, so our future approach should be going to where people already gather and somehow get them to say some words like, "I love Jesus". I have no idea why I told you all this, because this book is about neighbors, not the local dive. On top of that, it is about creating a Block Party of Salvation, not going to where people are already gathered. I guess I only bring it up because people have realized after being to enough of these 'cultural activities' in churches, the ulterior motive was always to get them to pray a prayer after being convinced they will burn eternally in hell if they don't!

A Simple Scriptural Mistreatment

I am still trying to convince you that Jesus combined loving God and loving your neighbors into one commandment, so I will l keep repeating that without any textual reference, and like my marketing consultant told me, by the end of the book I will be able to convince you that the Great Commandment Jesus spoke of is to love our literal neighbor as ourselves. So, lets just forget that big scary Bible and start doing what Jesus said to do, and that is to love our literal neighbors!

To make this point, we will not bother with any scriptural proof because the Bible can mean anything we want it to, so instead, our focus will lay in convincing our readers with emotional appeals. We begin with visualizing the horrible scene your neighborhood will become if you do not obey Jesus. If you do not intervene, the following will start to happen:

- *Isolation:* Our lives will progress down the rabbit hole of loneliness where we self-medicate with more late-night news and prescription drugs. We will soon forget we live on a block at all and regard the noises outside as the results of the zombie apocalypse.
- *Fear:* We will finally come to the true knowledge that our neighbors are the drunken child-flingers we always knew they were. Since we do not know our neighbors, and we fear what we do not know, logic says that these people living a mere fifty feet away terrify us and cause the reflex reaction of screaming and running every time we see another human on our block.
- *Misunderstanding:* When our neighbors start to bring down the property value by not mowing the lawn, we will automatically assume they are careless bums who cannot peel themselves off the television long enough

to take a sickle to the jungle outside. Not even code-enforcement can get these guys to mow the lawn!

Clearly, not loving the neighbor will ripple into horrible circumstances in the whole world, and *God wants us to love the way he loves*, this absolutely means we should drop everything and show up on the neighbors porch every day until he is worn out and helps with the block party (Luke 18:1-18).

Strangers Actually Showed Up

While our group started talking about this neighboring thing, my family was hosting a small group, but we only ever invited people from church, so the neighbors felt isolated and were fearful of the big group of people showing up at our house every week. They misunderstood our Bible study for a frat party and wondered if they should call the police. Anyway, I went all week without preparing anything for my weekly small-group Bible study. This was nothing new because I usually wait for God to impress something on my heart at the last minute, but this night I was too tired to think of something to call a message that 'God put on my heart' so I phoned my wife to have her just invite the group for a potluck instead. I don't really believe in this small group stuff anyway, and we could always just call it 'fellowship' because that word has such a broad and useless definition in the modern church.

But my wife, that rascally critter, invited all these strangers to our house without first asking my opinion. I did not realize they were my neighbors, but I did not care because I walked in the door to see some stranger I never saw before touching my guitar! Who was this space invader that he was on MY couch and touching MY guitar?!

I was totally upset by this imposition of my life! I was tired and did not want to work, have a small group, and certainly, I did not want to get to meet more people. After all, I spent all day dealing with people's problems, and here is a whole new crop of people to dump their lonely and fearful lives into my lap! I realized that I needed to intentionally lean into my missional responsibility to bring kingdom principles to these unsaved heathens. Yes, accommodating my neighbors takes extra work, and I may even have to learn to love people when I am not being paid to do it.

The Real Good Samaritan

In Luke 10, we find twelve painful verses about the Good Samaritan. I know that twelve verses is too much to read, I will condense it down to just a few sentences. This will serve my desire to twist the lawyer in the story to fit what you might be thinking right now, because that would create another emotional appeal to convince you that you must love your literal neighbor.

One day, an expert in the law wanted to know from Jesus how to inherit eternal life. This was not any normal lawyer, he was just like all of us! He was an isolated, fearful, misunderstanding person who was so self-centered he only associated with people just like himself so he was not accused of being a democrat. He was also so full of activities that he could have never found the time to plan, let alone attend a Block Party of Salvation. Now that I have set you up to be this guy, I will say that Jesus asks him a question, "What is written in the law?"

Since this lawyer is so much like us, we say, "I have no clue. I love Jesus, but I have never read the Bible." But since this was a story in the Bible and not an empty shell of you readers, the lawyer responded, "'Love the Lord your God with all your heart and with all your soul and with all your strength and with all your mind' and 'Love your neighbor as yourself.'" Unlike us, he knew the Bible well. Good thing my readers are not so well informed!

Anyway, Jesus says to go and do likewise. That was not good enough for the lawyer, he wanted to know the answer to his next question, the one we have teased you with, defined though emotion, but ignored the Bible. But alas, in our study for this material, Google showed us Luke 10:29, so we had to find a way to twist around so you can see Jesus defining 'neighbor' because it did not match our narrative. Here we go. If you get confused, it is just us making logical leaps to avoid the issue, don't worry about it; just trust us. We are pastors.

We first need to understand this lawyer wanted to define 'neighbor' in a way he could justify his actions and choose whom to love. This guy is like us! We are also trying to find a loophole in what Jesus said is the most important thing to do (trust us...loving your neighbor is the Great Commandment). Jesus answers the question by telling the parable of the Good Samaritan.

As a man was headed to Jericho he was beaten and robbed. A pastor walked by but seeing the bloody mess of a man, he said to himself, "I don't have time to stop and help this stranger in need. My literal neighbors need their Block Party of Salvation and my preparations are not complete". This happened twice. Finally a guy who was like the foreign guy down the street who speaks with an accent stopped and helped the man, cleaned him up and took him to a hospital (I know the Bible says Inn, but I am trying to make this dramatic). The point is clear: The Samaritan is the true neighbor because he was not focused on the literal neighbor at the time he encountered a person in need. Now, you see that what Jesus defines as a neighbor runs contrary to my narrative, so I will spend the whole next section invalidating who Jesus defines as a neighbor so I can later guilt trip you into throwing your own Block Party of Salvation.

Twisting Who My Neighbor Is

I know following the command to be flexible to the calling of God where you are does not conform to any three-point plan of salvation or scheme to get someone to hear your pastor talk about Jesus, so that is too inconvenient as a definition of *neighbor*. I mean, the Bible is an irrelevant 2000 year old book, so we have to modernize things. After all, our lives are too rushed and scheduled to stop to help at the scene of an accident. As long as we snap the photos with our cell phones to share on Facebook we are satisfied. But what we can all do is adjust our schedules to invite the literal neighbors over for burgers. I know, the heart in The Good Samaritan was to be flexible in all times of need, but again...the Bible is 2000 years old. We need to modernize things! If we take the Bible at face-value we will fall into the trap of defining our neighbor as anyone outside of the eight closest houses to us. With my formula, your neighbor is clearly defined: The people who only live within eight houses! Anyone outside of that is not your neighbor! I don't know why Jesus had to make this complicated.

After all, as we read this parable two thousand years later we turn the Samaritan into a metaphor, and that makes us numb to The Great Commandment. If we say that 'everyone' is my neighbor this somehow gives us an excuse to not follow The Great Commandment because we cannot possibly love 'everyone' all the time! I know, Jesus did not say, 'everyone is your neighbor', he said a neighbor is the person in need right where you are, but trust me, that means 'everyone at all times' and that is too broad. After all, shooting arrows at the broad side of a barn will mean we never hit the barn. I know that does not make sense, but trust me, Jesus's definition of neighbor is just too broad.

After two thousand years of this parable's meaning not being debated even by Catholics and Protestants, we are here to finally set the world straight by telling you we have been defining the man on the side of the road way too broad. While it might *appear* on the surface we need to help anyone we encounter with a need, that is too broad to be reality. Instead, your neighbor is only the people in the eight closest houses to you, so love those people or you are not obeying Jesus. You must know the real names, phone numbers, and addresses of those people or risk being excluded from the kingdom of God.

Burning Rubber!

We are going to try a quick exercise that is sure to lead you to an immediate conviction of the sin of failing to take The Great Commandment seriously. This exercise is called The Chart of Shame because it gives you healthy guilt about not successfully knowing the names and date of conversion for your eight closest neighbors. We will start by building a tic-tac-toe grid where you place your 'X' in the center grid because we all need to acknowledge that we are the center of the universe. Do not use a map of the neighborhood because that will remove the illusion that you are the center of all creation.

Now that your Chart of Shame is ready, write 'a', '2', and 'd' in each of the eight remaining grids where the 'X' or the 'O' would otherwise go. Fill these out as follows:

- a – Write the name of everyone in the house. If they are those strange people whom are never home or are like that guy who only enters and exits the house through the garage, you might need to peek through the windows to determine the number of people living there. I find it helpful to count beds, but watch out for guest bedrooms.

- 2 – Write down some relevant information about the people in the house that you cannot see by standing in the driveway. This can be a difficult task and takes some courage because I find I usually cannot fill this out without going through their garbage. Again, this cannot be something you can spot from the center of the universe in your driveway, but things you might have learned by talking to them could be helpful.

- d – Write down the date the person prayed to love Jesus. This does not need to be a time they really changed their life, we are merely looking for the date they said a shallow prayer in response to an emotional story about burning in Hell.

After administering The Chart of Shame in thousands of church services we have found that America is really bad at The Great Commandment. This is what we find:

- About 10 percent of people can fill out line 'a' without looking in the windows.
- About 3 percent of people can fill out line '2' without digging through the neighbor's garbage
- Less than 1 percent have led their neighbors to pray a prayer for Jesus or know when the neighbor did that.

Look at your pitiful results! Jesus commands us to love our literal eight neighbors, but we cannot even fill out this chart. Lean in to the knowledge that you will burn in hell for not having this chart filled out completely! But we also understand that Jesus said some crazy things about love and neighbors, including that our enemy should be a neighbor, and we need to go out of the way to be a neighbor, and sometimes we need to love people who are hostile toward us. But this is all out there, advanced graduate school love! We know we are all miserable saps who have a hard time putting down our guitars since it is evident we do not really love people. We will go back to kindergarten love. This means that we cannot love anyone else out there *until* we love the eight closest people on our block. After all, how could we possibly love an ISIS terrorist if we cannot first love the heathen, drunken child-flinger next door? It all boils down to this: If you are not loving the people in the eight closest house to yours, you are not obeying The Great Commandment.

Who Lives Next Door?

When my wife threw that party and invited all those strangers from next door, many of them said they wept aloud after seeing all these people filing into our apartment. They heard the raging party and they would have called the police for the noise violation but they were too busy crying in their own personal loneliness. But after tonight, people suddenly started to invite us to their house to talk about all their problems. Within a week we were helping a drug addict recover and a couple on the verge of divorce to reconcile their marriage. All this happened because we removed the fish sticker from our cars and replaced it with our magnetic Chart of Shame to show the world that we did not care about anyone but those in the eight closest houses to us.

3

TV is Taking my Time

As a society, we are horrible neighbors for two general reasons. First, shallow-minded people like me spend way too much time watching television. We have to know what happens on our programs, and missing those television shows induces catatonic stress into our lives. The second reason we may not neighbor well is we are so distracted by the things God has truly called us to do like serve in missions, teach Sunday school, or other great community projects like Big Brothers, Big Sisters. Some of us may even have our own ministries which do not conform to any of that normal stuff, but we reach people for Christ every day. Either way, if you are taking The Great Commandment seriously, you will certainly be convicted by your lack of ability in block party organization. I mean really, some of us already have meaningful relationships that we will have to shipwreck in order to get to know the people who live in the eight closest houses to us.

It is vital at this time to take a step back and examine our current commitments. If we are not getting to know our eight closest neighbors than we need to re-prioritize our life and drop those things God has called us to because Jesus defines our neighbors as those people in the eight closest houses to ours and if we cannot learn to love them, then we certainly cannot be expected to love those other people further away.

A challenge to this good neighbor stuff is our busy schedules. Our world requires us to become rats in wheels, answering emails in an ever-full inbox. I even once tried to stop and smell some roses, but my boss got all in my face about taking an unauthorized break, and to think, I do all this to make payments on the stuff I did not need and can not really afford. We all try to make ourselves look more successful than we really are, and usually we do it to impress our church group. I mean really, fifteen years ago did you dream you could:

- Illegally make phone calls while driving your car.
- Send email with your nose as you talk on speaker phone while driving with your knee.
- Have a DVR you could record all your favorite television shows so you can continue filling your mind with the crap Hollywood produces even when you are busy at the time it airs.
- See the screen of the people you are talking to, but keep Sudoku over top of it because you really do not want to be there, but it looks like you are, so this is better than the office!

If we really knew all that stuff was going to be happening we would have certainly doubled or even tripled the television shows that we record to spend even less time doing important things. We could even plan times to sit around the table as a family but be totally transfixed to our personal digital screens for hours and never say a word to each other.

Despite all this great technology we could use to make our lives more efficient, we have chosen instead to download a myriad of crappy games and sports apps so we can alleviate all hints of boredom in every spare, unstimulated second. As a result, we live in total chaos running from one deadline to the next because of the procrastination our technology enables in our lives! We live in *Ludicrous Speed* looking like multitaskers but really we are just playing Farmville while we look like we are being productive. The resultant busy schedule makes us push our kids off on day cares, schools, and church youth groups to raise instead of pawning them at the neighbors house for the day. We get home late at night and instead of doing something meaningful like reading the Bible we profess to love so much, we rather choose to watch more Hollywood filth we have saved on our ever-growing DVR save list, maybe pay some bills, and then we go to sleep and repeat that process day in and day out. These observations led me to three lies we all tell ourselves about our crazy life:

Lie #1 – *Someday I will be a good neighbor.* The truth is we will never be available to our eight closest neighbors until we quit our jobs and abandon the ministries God has truly called us to.

Lie #2 – *More Stuff will be enough.* We need to stop buying so much because the Jones's next door are caught in this one-upping contest. We both keep trying to compete with one another. He buys a new car, so I buy a newer car, he gets a John Deere, so I had to get the next pricier model. This has to stop! As long as we are trying to impress Mr. Jones, we will never get to love him!

Lie #3 – *Everybody is a rat in a wheel.* We seem to believe our culture requires everyone to be constantly busy. The real reason we are not good neighbors is because everyone is just too busy being the rat in the wheel, but some people have learned to overcome this. They are strange, though. They use their cell phones as tools rather than a bionic body part. They slow down and listen to God by studying his word and praying. I just do not have time for that.

The healthiest person who ever lived was Jesus. Even though he got tons of things done, he never seemed to be in a hurry. It was clear, he did not have a cell phone or a DVR to distract him in his life. He did want us to have a full life as he says in John 10:10, but I don't want to talk about what he did, because it was not with his eight closest neighbors.

I Don't Want to Decide

Anyone who knows me can tell sports are clearly more important to me than God. Though I might struggle with studying the Bible, it is easy for me eat, sleep, and breathe every sport that has ever existed! I love sports so much I dedicate a large portion of my daily life to memorizing sports statistics. My obsession with sports is so great I have imposed my will of loving baseball on my kids just like they must attend church, Awana, youth group, small group, even though it is meaningless to them. Now I force the kids into sports even more because I have taken up coaching again.

As a coach, I have learned that ability is important but repetition is more so. In fact, repetition is so important that I know if I repeat that The Greatest Commandment only means to love the eight closest households in your neighborhood, eventually you will even start to believe it! So the best way to do anything great is to do it over and over again. Taking our sports analogy, in order to make sure your kids know more about baseball than God, make sure you get him into the league early, get them into the best league, and make sure he never misses a practice! It takes lots of time and lots of money to turn your kid into a great athlete, and that is the most important thing your child can become!

Of course, we wanted to focus on the eight closest people to us, so we decided to dash our son's dreams of being the next Mike Trout. We decided to pull him from the league that would give him all of the practice and we put him into the local open league that would put him on teams with people in the eight closest houses to us. The point was clear: we should let go of our opportunities to reach our true potential to make sure the people in the eight closest houses to us were invited to a barbecue. Ultimately, we decided to not have our son grow into an athlete after all because we know the odds of going professional are low and the lifestyle was not conducive to block parties, so we made the decision to not have him reach his true potential.

Intentional Choices

Like in prior sections, we will not let our thoughts rest on you without totally contradicting what we have just said, so now we assume you do want your son to be the next Mike Trout, and since we know everyone has a different story and most people are too lazy to follow the practices of some book they read, we want to give you an out. We are not really teaching anything God has taught anyway, but, I need you to understand you risk an eternity in hell if you are not going to be a good neighbor, so some adjustments may be needed in your life. After all, Jesus often times stopped his planned schedule to placate some person whom was interrupting him. Want proof? Do you? Well, one day when Jesus was walking down the street some blind guy started calling to him. The disciples were reminding Jesus of his tight schedule, but Jesus stopped to talk to the man. He did the same thing when some parents where bringing him their children, when some guy wanted him to heal his daughter, and there was also some story about a woman with a health problem! I can't remember where any of those stories are in the Bible, and biblical analysis is too hefty a task for the modern Christian, so just take my word for it: Jesus interrupted his schedule so you can, too. After all, WWJD? We do know he was never in a hurry but got lots done. We must learn to focus exclusively on the people in the eight closest houses to our house!

We want to make the point further so I will quote from some 'neighboring church' pastor: "In this life, we can do only a few things really well; I think it's a good idea to make certain that one of those things is what Jesus says is most important.[1]" Of course, since Jesus was meaning that we need to love our literal neighbors, we need to prioritize our time to that end. Time spent surfing the internet, playing video games, or just watching reruns of sitcoms will amount to as much value as watching sports, memorizing statistics, but that is OK, because it is my passion! Regardless, you should cut out everything that gets in the way of loving your eight neighbors including any ministry you were called to serve.

Good, Great, and Godly

Our life is a series of choices and often times we need to let go of some good things in order to get the great things. The story of Mary and Martha in Luke 10 is about two sisters who are both doing good things, but Mary chose better things because she is listening to Jesus rather than working. Martha wants Jesus to tell Mary to help her in the kitchen but Jesus replies:

> "Martha, Martha," the Lord answered, "you are worried and upset about many things, but few things are needed—or indeed only one. Mary has chosen what is better, and it will not be taken away from her (Luke 10:41-42)."

Of course, this means that sometimes we need to say no to some good things like the evening news in order to do the better thing like throwing a block party. This was definitely not a lesson about letting distractions like block party preparations get in the way of learning from the word of God. We don't need to study the pages of the Bible as long as we 'Love Jesus', whatever that means. We will be expected to let go of everything that is not loving the people in those eight closest houses so we can show our love through a block party.

More Neighbor Time Today

Relationships are important and maybe we are already spending time on good relationships spawned out of the circumstances in our life like Jesus suggested we should do. We may even be friends with people at work or the parents of our child's extracurricular activities. Some of us might even have friends from long ago whom are important to us. But while those relationships are good, I must impress on you the importance of misinterpreting what Jesus said by making a new command called The Great Commandment, which is to only love the people in eight closest houses to where we live. We cannot be friends with those in convenient locations like work, and we must stop the calling God gave us to so we can connect with those literally next door. I know that The Good Samaritan was about loving those who were close to where we find ourselves situationally, but I want to suggest that the term *neighbor* is too broad to include anyone outside our immediate literal neighborhood. After all, if we love the people in the world, we are spreading our love too thin and we need to readjust our definition so we only love people who literally live close to us.

If we can not find the time to love our literal neighbors, we are wretched sinners and need to eliminate the non-essentials. Here are three principles I have identified to help find more time for those eight families we are too busy to spend our time focusing on.

First, we need to *Make the Eight Closest Houses the Main Thing*. This means anything getting in the way of planning the Block Party of Salvation needs to go. We cannot take time being friends with our co-workers, and we should pull our children out of their activities because the next-door neighbor is not a co-participant. We need to abandon the call God gave us to free up time to hang out with the people on our block. Ultimately, we need to intentionally prioritize our life by putting God first (I have no idea what this means - I just heard it is important), putting family second, and finally, putting what Jesus said was important in the third place: Loving our literal neighbor by throwing a block party.

Secondly, we need to *Eliminate Time Wasters* like everything not aligned with getting to know the neighbor. I will suggest to eliminate television, games, and the internet until the neighbor comes over to do those activities with us. Study that tic-tac-toe board we created in chapter 2 and eliminate everything not related to that board.

Finally, *Be Interruptible – but Only by Your Neighbor*. We are all so totally self-centered it is nearly impossible to let the whims of someone else get in the way of our actions. Of course, this only applies to anyone in the eight closest houses because anyone outside that range would constitute a definition of *neighbor* too broad for our elementary definition of love to include.

A Science not an Art

One time I was invited to two parties on the same night. It put me into horrible *paralysis of analysis* because I really wanted to go to the party with my old college buddies I have been friends with for years. But we had made a commitment to get to know the neighbors and of all days they would finally acquiesce it was a night I had a party to attend. I really wanted to see the good friends whom have been in my life for years, and I actually have things in common with those guys. But we had this nagging commitment to get to know the neighborhood so we had to go to that party. I made the decision to first go to the college party for a few hours and then go to the neighborhood party. I know that is the best of all worlds, worked perfectly fine, and it allowed me to maintain old friendships while I forged ahead with new ones, but logically living our life in balance is not the point of this book.

To make my point about prioritizing I will just declare that I 'interrupted' (see how I tied that into the last point?) my plans to see the college friends to get to know the neighbors. Was my plan to see both groups good? Yep! But that would fly in the face of my narrative so I will instead say that we skimmed the surface at both parties. It was *good* to go to the college party but it was *better* to go to the neighborhood party. In other words, an art is something that takes practice and it's a little subjective. We want to be objective, so neighboring is a science, not an art. It is not about balancing life, it is about forsaking everything that is not related to the neighborhood relationships, and that gives us a perfect scientific formula. The formula is simple: reprioritize your life to always be at home waiting to fill needs of those in the eight closest houses, have courage to plan a block party, and let go of everything interfering with our plan. Do these things and you will live at a pace that proves you take the Great Commandment literally.

4

The Fear of the Neighborhood Psycho

hen my wife and I first moved into our new neighborhood, we felt the piercing eyes of the total strangers on our new block but we realized they would probably not make the first move at introductions, so we baked fresh apple pies to help us break the neighbors' icy glares. Most people took the pies with total suspicion, sniffing them and wondering if we could be trusted. Others were embarrassed because they came to the door in their underwear, but one man in a turban saw us coming and took off running in the other direction. I think he yelled 'ali akbar' as he ran, but I could not tell under his thick accent. We almost caught up to him, but his door closed as we ran up the stairs to his front porch. We pounded on the door, but he would only answer us through the mail slot. He was afraid, however, because he thought we were trying to sell him pies while we stuffed religious literature down his pants. He screamed at us several times to just leave, but we were bound and determined to deliver our diabetic payload of roasted apples in a golden, flaky crust. We left the pie at his door and hid in the bushes watching while he poked the pie with a stick, wondering if it would explode. We wondered what would make a man act so erratically.

My wife and I discussed the incident, devastated because we could not understand this guy. He certainly talked with an accent, so we thought that our American forwardness was over the top crazy. Perhaps everyone ignored this guy because of his turban and accent, or maybe he was so bothered by the constant barrage of salespeople, he rejects all strangers. Either way, we were totally confused by his behavior.

A few days later I saw the turban-laden man outside doing yard work. I slowly and cautiously approached him with my hand outstretched in a gesture of friendliness. I introduced myself as a new neighbor and this time he was more receptive. He recalled 'the pie incident' the other day but believed we were salespeople. Our relationship had a rocky beginning. We made a point to wave at him if we saw him around the block, but he never waved back...until that one fateful day! We rejoiced in ABSOLUTE JUBILATION! GOD WAS ON THE MOVE! It was a great day when he waved back! Later, he confessed he was afraid of us, but changed his mind in response to all the smiles and waves!

My Addiction to News

I am not surprised by the fear and suspicion among our neighbors. We choose to watch non-stop, fear-inducing bad news on our televisions, computers, tablets, and phones. And though we could turn it off, we just sit transfixed to the syndicated sins, failing to realizing the negative impact such programming has on our outlook on life. Excessive exposure to the news finally illuminates the sick and broken world surrounding us, and we start to see the neighborhood as an extension of that evil. It is our task as Jesus-loving perfect people is to bring the neighborhood into utopia and the best way to do that is to get people to pray to love Jesus, and the best way to do that is to figure out how to talk to the freaky neighborhood psycho.

When we start considering those psychos, here are some people we are right to be suspicious toward:

- You might have a single neighbor who is a man and you have prejudice toward single people in general, but men in particular.
- Your kids have neighborhood friends but their parents never said a little prayer to love Jesus so you feel uneasy about your offspring going over there.
- One family on the block clearly lives there, but they never seem to be home. Who has a house but doesn't live there?
- Maybe you are just apprehensive about getting to know people because you cannot escape the ever-calling voice of Mr. Wilson every time you are trying to grill up some burgers. If you take the time to neighbor well, you will find yourself always at the mercy of

these people you can never escape...except those weirdos who have the house but are never home.

Of course not all fear is bad. If you approach one specific house to deliver an apple pie and you see a pentagram drawn upon the floor in blood you are probably wise to steer clear or call the authorities, but most of this fear stuff is just an obstacle to obeying the Great Commandment.

Even if you find yourself at a drunken neighborhood party, children running wild, some guy in the corner is dancing with a lamp shade on his head, no matter what, be intentional and lean into the fact that by simply being there you are obeying the Great Commandment. After all, attending such a party will bring you closer to God somehow. I am not sure how, but just trust me, I'm a pastor!

Giant Grasshoppers

The Israelites were worldly people who really wanted to enter the land of Canaan but their feet froze at the border of the promised land out of absolute, terrifying fear. Numbers 13 tells their story. Twelve spies were sent to scout out the land but ten of them came back terrified of what they saw. They loved the land, don't get me wrong. They said it was fantastic including waterfalls of milk and bees just dropped off honey to people like they do in *Dora the Explorer*, but giant grasshoppers also lived in the land! The ten fearful spies focused so much on those giant grasshoppers they convinced the rest of the people that going into the land meant horrible death.

Two spies, Joshua and Caleb, knew the fear was getting in the way of God's provision, after all, no one ever directly inter-

viewed the giant grasshoppers. If they did, they would have realized the grasshoppers were really terrified of the Israelites!
Instead, God's people were fearful and so they missed out on
the great things God really wanted them to have.

After forty years the people came once again to the border of Canaan but only two spies were sent out this time...any
more than that and the people come back terrified again. This
time, however, the spies came to a resident who explained
years earlier how paralyzed in fear the people were. To prove
it, I will quote from this verse totally out of context:

"I know that the Lord has given you this land and that a great
fear of you has fallen on us, so that all who live in this country
are melting in fear because of you. We have heard how the Lord
dried up the water of the Red Sea for you when you came out of
Egypt, and what you did to Sihon and Og, the two kings of the
Amorites east of the Jordan, whom you completely destroyed.
When we heard of it our hearts melted in fear and everyone's
courage failed because of you, for the Lord your God is God in
heaven and on the earth below (Joshua 2:9-11)."

It is unmistakable. The Israelites should have come into
the land the first time, but they were afraid of their neighbors
and only thought they were giant grasshoppers. The neighbors
also feared God's people because of the things they heard he
had done. Fear has a way of distorting our perceptions and we
start to become afraid of each other. This is the same when we
look at our neighborhoods. When we know we are on God's
mission we can lean in and be intentional to go out into our
neighborhoods and rescue our neighbors from the fear of block
parties!

Of course, God is not an all-protecting force! We need to learn to balance our fears with a healthy dose of intelligence. You may very well stand in front of your neighbor's house ringing the doorbell only to find yourself on Hannibal Lecter's front porch! Be careful, and be like Daniel: avoid the meat (Daniel 1:12). But there is also a part of our fear which is not justifiable and we need to pick up our missional cross and walk with it. Life is not always safe, and seeking safety means we are not following Jesus, but we need to push through all the irrational fear and drop off that freshly baked apple pie! Who cares if your neighbor thinks you are weird, as long as they attend the block party!

Playing in the Front Yard

Tim and Angelica lived in the same house for over a decade but lived like hermits. They did not know anyone else on the cul-de-sac of eight houses. They really wanted to know their neighbors, but the thought of going and knocking on doors just to say hi was a terrifying prospect to this young couple, but no one was coming over to their house to make the first move. After several years of waves and smiles, Tim finally had enough and decided it was time to finally do something different, something scary, something terrifying.

They realized they were timid people and that made them apprehensive about making the first step. Much like all of us, Tim and Angelica were socially afraid, and after being in the same cul-de-sac with the same people for so long, they did not want to suddenly make the first move because the neighbors would fear they either found religion or joined Amway.

Tim finally decided the reason they were social hermits is they were using the back yard so the neighbors could not see them doing things outside. The solution was simple: switch yards. With the social hub of the family being converted to the front yard, the neighbors would need to awkwardly smile and wave more often, but the trap was set! While they set up chairs to lay in wait for their victims of neighborly conversation, the children played in view of other children and eventually some other neighborhood kids came over to play. This of course forced the neighbors to make the first move. They had to come over to make sure their children were not playing among psychopaths, and this setup meant Tim and Angelica could maintain their fear and timidity but setup a trap of which their own children were the bait. So you can keep your spirit of timidity, just move to the front yard!

Once a quorum of neighbors had been made acquaintances, Tim set out to create the Block Party of Salvation. Barriers were broken down and neighbors started to know the names of the other people in the cul-de-sac. They even started inviting one another into each other's houses! Neighbors helped neighbors and world peace broke out, marriages were saved, and a little girl came home to a neighbor's house instead of being a horrible latch-key kid coming home alone every day. Once Tim and Angelica moved from the back yard to the front yard, God was on the move creating real neighbors who took the Great Commandment seriously.

5

The Next House in Line

Once, I tried to work from home but like everyone else in the world, I tend to procrastinate. I looked out the window and observed the neighbor working on a car I had never seen in his driveway before. I don't know anything about cars, so I went out to talk to Dale since it afforded me the opportunity to both procrastinate and snake my way into his business. I closed the computer lid and went outside. My conversation with Dale lasted for a long time and in the process I learned the car belonged to his son. Both the car and the kid were having problems so I was able to tell him that Jesus could make all his problems go away. This was the catalyst for a great conversation, and now we each know the dates we each professed to love Jesus. All I had to do is walk outside when I was supposed to be working!

Becoming a good neighbor is a lot like cleaning the extended household-junk storage locker, sometimes called a garage. Our lives are so shallow we buy excess stuff and when our stuff does not fulfill us, we toss it into the garage to make room for more stuff. Once we have accumulated so much of this stuff in the garage, it becomes an insurmountable challenge to clean the place out. Just like cleaning the garage, knocking on the neighbor's house to get to know them is an insurmountable task. But if we learn to procrastinate, we can tackle the easy steps to becoming a neighbor that would make Jesus proud!

To understand how this process will work, I have developed an extraordinary simple flow diagram to demonstrate how friendships work:

Strange Acquaintance → Guy You Wave To → Backyard Buddy

Strange Acquaintances

When we built our tic-tac-toe board in chapter 2 and tried to enter the names of the people in the eight houses closest to ours, we may have found some blanks where we could not enter any names without going through the trash. Those people are called 'strangers', meaning people whom we have not yet made our acquaintance. We may have waved at them, and if they wave back, they are potential new friends, but to move to the phase of backyard buddy, we need to take the next step!

In order to take the Great Commandment seriously and become the type of neighbor Jesus will let into heaven, we need to learn the neighbor's name. If you are anything like me, you can't remember names because you are too focused on yourself. I mean, no one in the world can remember names for longer than 30 seconds and the whole country should be on Ritalin; after all, that would make the pharmaceutical companies very happy!

We may have met many of our neighbors in the past, but have forgotten their names. So how do we get those names back once you have forgotten them? I will give you two possible fool-proof plans. First, the hard one is to go up and ask for their name again. Feel free to tell the neighbor how bad your memory is so you do not feel like a total jerk for not knowing if they are Mike or Bob. They will likely reciprocate unless they think you found religion or joined Amway in which case they might lie about their name. The less embarrassing and often more accurate method of deriving a person's name is to wait until about 2:00 AM on trash day and go through their garbage, but watch out for improperly labeled junk mail. Once you have their name again, make sure you write it down. In order to streamline this process, we sell a magnetic dry-erase tic-tac-toe board to post on your refrigerator. Be sure to write down the names as soon as you have them so you do not have to admit that you forgot their name again. Once you have their names, be sure to commit them to memory. After all, you make your kids memorize the Awana verses, but we are talking about wanting to please Jesus by obeying The Great Commandment, so memorizing the neighbor's names will prove how much we love Jesus.

Strange Friends

Now that we know our neighbor's name we must make them our backyard buddy. After all, in the Parable of the Good

Samaritan, the man who was beaten along the path and the Samaritan man who helped him became the best buds and even started throwing block parties to save the Pharisee and Levite who left him bloody on the road to Jericho. The point is, in order to love anyone we have to move beyond the realm of casual wavers and become best buddies. Without being a best buddy, we cannot love anyone.

Converting our relationship from the guys who wave to each other into backyard buddies is not as easy as asking their name or digging through their garbage. To help you, we will once again forget we have a Bible that is useful for instruction about living our faith and once again consult with a secular city manager. The manager we consulted this time has read the same buzz-word filled books we have so it was no surprise she challenged us to, "Lean in to equip your congregations for the missional task of enabling relational on-boarding though a frictionless deep-dive into the intentional challenging of the congregation's paradigm about neighboring which will move the needle towards equipping the people into the kingdom-focus to throw block parties." We were once again totally in awe of this demi-god for telling us about the power of block parties. We took her words to heart and started measuring our congregation's commitment to Jesus by how many block parties they threw.

When we talk about block parties, we are not talking about HOA parties, because those parties are not our parties. I know, they are both organized by the same people, living in the same community and exclusively for the people in the community, and in fact, they might even have more funding because of those HOA fees. But trust us, our block parties will be attended by everyone, not just 10% of the neighborhood. How do I know that? Because Jesus.

Block parties are the most important place to become backyard buddies with the guys you wave to. The block party provides a casual environment where we can talk to people we already know, and if we decide to break out of our already familiar clique of backyard buddies, we might even meet someone new! This is a natural place to meet our neighbors, and this is why Jesus spent so much time at parties! Here is a Bible story that will certainly not demonstrate how much Jesus loved parties, but I can twist it to fit into my shallow narrative, so head on over to Luke 5:27-32:

> "After this, Jesus went out and saw a tax collector by the name of Levi sitting at his tax booth. 'Follow me,' Jesus said to him, and Levi got up, left everything and followed him. Then Levi held a great banquet for Jesus at his house, and a large crowd of tax collectors and others were eating with them. But the Pharisees and the teachers of the law who belonged to their sect complained to his disciples, 'Why do you eat and drink with tax collectors and sinners?' Jesus answered them, 'It is not the healthy who need a doctor, but the sick. I have not come to call the righteous, but sinners to repentance.'"

This huge volume of scripture contains so much we could write a whole book on this topic. Of importance is that Levi threw a party that would make frat boys look like boy scouts, and Jesus was happy to show up, even though he knew he would be criticized by the religious leaders. Ultimately, Jesus had no problem going to this party attended by sinners and prostitutes, but other people looked at him as if he were doing something wrong.

The same will happen to us. If we attend frat-like parties where the keg flows and people are engaged in all manner of immorality, our actions will be questioned by the perfect Christians in church, but do not let that distract you. When we engage such a party we are being just like Jesus regardless of how things go. After all, we can use that party as a way to weasel our way into the lives of these miserable wretches so we can save them. As Christians, we should be so worldly that we can throw the best block parties in the neighborhood, not criticizing the neighborhood gatherings because the music is loud and full of 'F' words.

Digging for Gold

Debbie was a secluded hermit who lived on her block for more than a decade without putting forth any effort to learn her neighbor's names. It was shocking to her that this neighborhood was nothing like the place she lived as a child when people were not too timid to say, "Hi there. By the way, I am Tom, what is your name?" so she lived a terrible, lonely life. One day, however, her church presented our fabulous material about creating shallow relationships with our eight closest houses so naturally, God chose that very day to tell her in spirits and a vision it was time to do something about this secluded neighborhood! She did something totally radical! She took out a piece of paper and drew upon it a large tic-tac-toe board, becoming devastated when she realized she had never taken a few minutes to just get to know her neighbor's names.

She sought God again and he spoke audibly that she just needs to go out and take walks looking for opportunities to introduce herself to her neighbors. There was this one neighbor that graciously exchanged waves on many occasions, so Debbie figured this was the perfect time to stop and talk to her. Debbie was so shocked that neighbor had so much in common with her own life. They both thought the block was so busy no one could introduce themselves, and they were both cancer survivors. What are the odds? This led to more conversations and Debbie learned this old widow had so many stories Debbie's mind just started spinning in circles. It was amazing what life stories are around us if we just go say 'Hi' to the people on our block!

Debbie had realized that every time we go and introduce ourselves to a neighbor it is like digging for gold. Sure, we will find some neighbors like that creepy single man who watches you every day at the coffee shop, but we might just be living next to someone who can teach we tons about life! It is like winning the lottery or finding a vein of gold, but we will not get the idea about saying hello to a neighbor without reading this awesome book on neighboring!

Of course, this is not the end of Debbie's amazing story, because God audibly spoke to her again goading her toward throwing a Block Party of Salvation. She printed up a Flier of the Gospel of Truth that outlined a plan for this party and distributed these fliers door-to-door as an excuse to fill out the names on her tic-tac-toe board. Within a month, God was on the move and Debbie stood in front of her driveway looking over more than forty neighbors who were all gathered together because she loved Jesus enough to throw a Block Party of Salvation!

You can see that all Debbie needed to do was follow the simple steps in this book to convert a group of forty hermits into backyard buddies by simply learning their names and inviting them into a Block Party of Salvation. Can you imagine what would happen if you were the courageous hero who organized the block party? You should commit to throwing at least one party per year, because if you don't, you are not being like Jesus! If you are an introvert, that is no problem. We will take away all your excuses. Here is what you need to do: 1.) Fill in your tic-tac-toe board; 2.) Plan a block party; 3.) Sit back and wait for good things to happen. Follow that simple plan and you will be ushering souls to the front of the line in heaven through your very own Block Party.

6

Infant Crawls

nyone can be a good neighbor, but just to prove how lame you are if you do not organize block parties I will tell you about an 11 year old boy name Nicky. This young boy's family made the commitment to dedicate their whole life to the eight houses nearest theirs and by happenstance a poor single mother with her seven foster kids lived right across the street! Wow! What an opportunity for an 11 year old boy to show us all up because he was there to help calm the chaos by tutoring the younger children in their schoolwork. What an example of how we should be neighboring! If an eleven year old boy can figure this stuff out, than surely all of us are without excuse.

I realize this book has been very long and boring so I want to take an interlude to discuss movies! We are so totally obsessed with movies in our culture we give more money to Hollywood than we do our missionaries, we spend more time watching movies than we do serving God, thinking about God, praying, and Bible study combined, but that is OK because *I'm OK, You're OK*, and we all love Jesus! But the type of neighboring I am talking about is not the sort of plot line we would expect in a movie we pay to see. The missional task of neighboring is boring because we merely identify our neighbors, invite them over, and become backyard buddies. But in reality, that is exactly what we need to do! After all, Jesus says being a good neighbor is exactly the kind of life that can change the world!

We do not need to be a superhero from a movie, but we do need to learn to give. By giving, we are able to allow God the room to do a miracle and if we can just find a few minutes a week to give, God will give us back so many blessings. Go ahead and test him on that! He always uses the small things we bring to him to create miracles. If you don't believe me then keep reading and I will prove it by paraphrasing and adding more into Bible verses than they really say.

Test God with Your Giving

The Bible contains a story about a hero so well known he is beyond naming in the text. This hero is so large he only merits a single verse. He gave his measly five barley loaves and two fish to Jesus because the crowd needed to be fed. Jesus charged the disciples with feeding the herd of people surrounding him, but the disciples did not have sufficient food or money. They brought this boy to Jesus because he had more than they did.

Our commitment to the Great Commandment is much like Jesus telling us to feed thousands of people. I mean, really, how can we be expected to remember some people's names or overcome the terror it takes to knock on a neighbor's door, right? We try to prioritize our time, but there is always someone new on that Hollywood stage being judged by morally bankrupt characters! We are trying to be like Jesus by loving people, but this is just too hard, much like ourselves trying to feed thousands of people.

But we need to lean into our Bible story. Just like this boy, when we give small sacrifices, God will multiply our time or bread into a miracle! He is able to turn something very small into something so great no one could have imagined it! In this case, Jesus performed a miracle where all of the people were fed from this boy's food. This model proves that Jesus will always give in abundance when you give all you have. Just keep giving everything away and he will keep filling you up. If you do not give, you will never expect to see a miracle.

Just Do It

This neighboring stuff is not just for other people. It is easy to think no one can knock on doors and invite people over except a few super Christians, but remember that when we offer small things to God, he will turn those things into miracles. In order to prime the pump for God's miracles we need to start knocking on doors and asking people's names! We never know which door will be our best backyard buddy, so just do it!

We realize it is difficult to divine neighborly activities, so we will help you out with two ideas you can build on for your specific situation:

- Those whom identify with being a woman can bake! Ideas include baking pies and taking them to the neighbor's house. If you are feeling particularly brave, you could even invite the neighbor back to your house to endeavor baking something together. Make sure you only do this with another person who identifies with being a female, because the women should do the cooking.

- Those whom identify with being a man, one word: Sports! It is a well known fact every man, without exception, is into all manner of sports. Invite the other male-identifying neighbors to play or watch sports! You could sit down talking about your favorite athlete or recite stats like your kids are made to recite Awana verses. This opens up all sorts of games for every season. Added bonus, the women could then bake cookies to serve to the men while they are engaging in 'fellowship'.

It can be intimidating to invite neighbors over, but in reality, most people on the block are probably all watching the same things on the television, but the neighbors may even have a better TV. My neighbor, Frank, has a television so large, it's screen is larger than my screen on my couch. Also, his wife, Annette, bakes the best lemon meringue pies ever, so why not invite the whole block to watch Frank's 2000 inch TV while eating Annette's pie. This way, everyone can become corrupted by Hollywood in the same place!

Don't assume people are too busy to want to join into television programming together. The neighbors are totally starved for attention but are lonely and crying because no one is inviting them over for dinner and televised, syndicated sin.

It is up to us to be intentional at filling out the tic-tac-toe board, knocking on the door, and starting the block party movement. Sometimes our relationship with the neighbors can move beyond pies and pig skin and we can start sharing our skills. Those mechanically inclined folks and contractors will have the endless opportunity to serve their neighbors by fixing cars and basement steps for free! This is especially handy since it helps with the goal of keeping the neighbor coming back for more free stuff. That extra time can be used to tell them about how much we love Jesus and offer the free gift! We will talk more about that in the next chapter. For now, remember, just do it!

7

Motives are Confusing

We realize our neighboring strategy is a radical approach to evangelism, but if we come off looking like an evangelist we risk scaring the neighbors away. We should initially keep our evangelistic goals a secret. If we follow the simple principles in this book, however, people who don't love Jesus will absolutely pray to love him and volumes of people will make it into heaven because of our efforts. God NEEDS us!

The reason I warn about trying to come off as an evangelist is our churches have gathered too many sales tactics from the business sector including high-pressure sales pitches. If we find ourselves saying things like, "Say this little prayer or you will burn in hell", we risk over-selling our love for Jesus. I know that our churches have taught us to use the ABCs of salvation, but this approach weirds people out when used too early in the relationship. We need to come up with a better approach, so let's look at another way.

A Better Word for Ulterior

In order to convince ourselves that we do not have the ulterior motive of strong-arming our neighbors to love Jesus, we will use the word, 'Ultimate', in place of 'Ulterior'. This is why:

> *Ulterior* means the task for converting our neighbor is hidden. We know our intent is to bring people to love Jesus because God needs our help, but that sounds very manipulative and the word, 'ulterior' generally has negative connotations in our society.
>
> *Ultimate* means the task for converting our neighbor is hidden, because we have not got there yet. We know our intent is to bring people to love Jesus, but ultimate is a much better sounding word in our society than ulterior, so we use 'ultimate' instead.

To clarify, we need to get our neighbors to profess to love Jesus. Our ulterior motive is never to share the gospel but our ultimate motive is always to share the gospel. Got it?

Our task is to drop our plans of evangelizing through block parties. Many think that every contact with another human is an opportunity to ask them to pray to love Jesus, and that is understandable. Our churches have taught us that whatever we do, the goal is to get someone to 'respond' to the gospel by saying a prayer in the same way Charles asked them to come forward. These are great motives and we also want everyone to profess to love Jesus because only he has the answers to all our problems. But Jesus does not call us to use bait-and-switch to get people into a block party only to get them to love Jesus, we should just love our neighbors because we love Jesus. So where does all that 'ultimate' motive stuff fit in? We will look at that next.

Door to Door Salesmen

I must confess the most remarkable situations find me. I can only assume God wants me to use my experiences as filler material for shallow books. I know the following story sounds so fantastic you might not believe it is real, but trust me, I am not making this stuff up! It all started one day when I was determined to throw a Block Party of Salvation. The plans were finalized, the date was set, we just needed to invite the neighbors. We printed up Fliers of the Gospel of Truth and cast a wide net around the eight closest houses to ours.

As we were pounding the pavement on our quest for neighborly connections, we encountered two other people in the neighborhood also out peddling their spiritual agenda. First we saw Jehovah's Witnesses knocking on every door, leaving behind those Watchtower pamphlets for those people afraid to answer the door. Once the JWs left, we shot up right behind them in the effort to offer a true religious offer: a Block Party of Salvation. No one was coming to the door even though we knew people where home. Those crazy JWs were scaring everybody away, because why would the people in those houses not come to the door to talk to us about our block party? They were simply avoiding the door because those other religious nut jobs were canvasing the neighborhood.

That very hour we also met another weirdo! He lived in the ninth house from us, so he was technically a neighbor but we did not know him. We did not even hand him an invitation, but he wanted to give my three sons a present. I am not usually inclined to let strange men give my kids gifts, but because we were trying to be good neighbors I said it was OK, while silently praying he was not handing out poisoned candy or some noisy toy. He gave a gay smile and silently laughed as he went back to his car procuring some colorful cube-like thing. The man then went on to describe this thing to be an EvangeCube that shows the three easy steps to start loving Jesus. I was totally buggered to see this guy trying to tell my kids about Jesus without first inviting them to a block party! This EvangeCube could not possibly work...it is just like those easy steps to salvation, but it was not *my* three easy steps so I stood there in awkward silence while this guy wove a web of hell so terrifying I was ready to profess my love for Jesus again just to be safe!

I broke the awkward silence with an awkward sentence detailing my occupation as pastor of the local shallow congregation. Furthermore, I lived in this neighborhood so how could he possibly not know that he was trying to convert a pastor's kids to some easy-believism Christianity without a block party? But in the course of the conversation I found out this weirdo walks the streets stopping everyone he sees, giving them an EvangeCube without ever assessing the degree they love Jesus, or even inviting them to a block party.

If those two different encounters were not enough, a third fantastic situation centered around yet another person that same hour! This neighbor wanted to know why we were having a party, so I told him all the reasons: connections, that everyone feels totally isolated and really wants to know one another, that the mayor is pushing the churches to do this neighborhood initiative, and more. "Ultimately", I said, "If enough neighborhoods around this town throw block parties than world peace will break out right here." Finally, however, the guy asked what I did for a living because that is what we do in this culture. As usual, as soon as I said I was a pastor he stiffened up like the platoon company when the drill sergeant enters the room. Suddenly my great idea of a block party turned sour as he realized this was a church outreach by a pastor. I was not sure if I was coming off as having the same motives as the EvangeCube guy or the Jehovah's Witnesses. After all, those people clearly had intentions of forcing their religion, but mine seemed sneaker, like there was an ~~ulterior~~ ultimate motive involved.

You can see why I said the most remarkable things happen to me. In the short course of a day this remarkable story unfolded so I could providentially write stories about how people knocking on doors to hand out religious literature is too pushy but weirdos with EvangeCubes are totally strange. Both of these people have good intentions, but there is clearly a better way. Rather than being direct with our approach to show people how much we love Jesus, we should throw a block party instead so we can realize our ultimate motive after we have built our relationship with people because friends have a hard time closing the door in our face when we start talking about Jesus.

Learning to Strong Arm Your Neighbor

For most of us, telling people how much we love Jesus is difficult. Often times we do not know how we are going to begin that process so we either withdraw from the Great Commission and risk people going to hell or we wrestle them to the ground until they profess to love Jesus. But there is a better way to make sure the neighbors profess to love Jesus, and the best part about it is it does not involving knowing anything about that big leather book. We just need a little pop psychology instead!

When we are in relationships with other people we naturally want to share the things that we love, and those people, because they are polite and consider themselves friends, will not just shut the door in our face. In my case, spending any amount of time around me will tell you I am so addicted to golf you would think I worship on the greens! The goal should be to accumulate friends with whom we start progressively talking more about Jesus. The more we love Jesus, the more he will come up in our conversations. Of course, if we neither love the neighbors nor Jesus, we will not start talking about him.

Talking about Jesus is easy. We just need to recognize our life is a story, and lasting relationships begin by telling our story. After all, the Bible itself is a series of stories. There are no clear principles to guide us in the Bible, just stories telling how miserable wretches like us came to love Jesus. Just like we have a story, however, our neighbors also have a story that they are longing to tell. Deep down inside, everyone wants to share their story and everyone longs for knowing how their story connects to other people's stories, and they may even start wondering if their story will connect with God's story, too.

In order to learn about strong-arming our neighbor we will talk about the four stages of conversation. First, we always talk about the things we see. These visible things include the weather or a snide comment about the other neighbor's ugly house...just to see if our present neighbor is into the same gossip we are into. These topics will lay some groundwork to be empowered to say "hi" to a total stranger who lives in one of the eight closest houses. Second, we talk about personal information. These conversational starters include how long the neighbor has lived on the block or where they grew up. We might even ask if the hooligans walking across the lawn every day belong to him. Most people are OK answering these types of questions and the answers help us determine how their story connects with God's story. When all the small talk is out of the way, the next stage in the evolution of conversation is to talk about hopes and dreams. A good friend will talk about his dreams and desires, so use this as a gauge to determine if this neighbor is a candidate for an 'ultimate discussion'. A person who is not friendly is not generally inclined to share their personal dreams, so once we hear those dreams we will be able to determine if this person is ready for the truth.

The final stage of conversation is the most important: try to talk with the neighbor about any regrets and pains in their lives. Be sure to avoid trivial things like back pain. We are looking for emotional pains, things that we can throw back into their face when when preparing to engage the ~~ulterior~~ ultimate motive of loving Jesus. Using these pains and problems, we are able to tell them how our problems and pains were much the same until we prayed to love Jesus. Once we did that, everything bad in our life vanished. When the neighbor hears how our story and their story overlap, their mind will jump through hoops recalling our personal love for Jesus vanquished our problems, and since our story overlaps with their story, they will realize professing love for Jesus will keep them out of hell, and dissolve their worldly problems! This is better than that two-for-one bologna deal at the local supermarket!

To Hear is to Obey

It is critical to talk about Jesus if we want to be good neighbors. If we are not talking to the people in the eight closest houses to ours we are just not obeying the Great Commandment. If we are really converted we will be talking to those people even if they never believe in Jesus, but our ~~ulterior~~ ultimate motive is always to tell them about the deep things in our heart, and that means telling them how much we love Jesus, whatever that means. We find that once we become friends with our neighbors, we start sharing sports and cooking, then that ultimate motive can come out. Once this occurs, pour out your heart about how much you love Jesus. That is the best way to share your faith.

Mike once told us a story about how this level of obedience lead him to organize a Block Party of Salvation that ultimately restored marriages and created a microcosm of world peace. Here is what he said.

"Our neighborhood became the center of world peace last summer when we decided to have a block party. I felt like a Baptist knocking on everyone's door and asking if they could come to a potluck and finding out what they would be bringing. Almost everyone showed up to the party, and no one was poisoned!

"That summer is when everyone's problems faded away. Although a few people did not work at building relationships, those who were obedient to the Great Commandment forged ahead into deeper friendships. One couple was struggling with their marriage and the mere attendance at our block party allowed us to talk about how much we loved Jesus and we were trying to convince them to love Jesus, too, because that would make all their problems go away. Eventually they started going to church and started to pray for me! Wow! God's kingdom is just breaking out all over the place because of our block party.

"Thanks to our block party, hermits on our street finally left their houses and got to know all the strangers in the eight closest houses. Sure, most people on the block are still heathens who do not profess to love Jesus, but there is hope! God may want to work in those relationships but his hands are tied until we all act and start our very own Block Party of Salvation!"

Mike's story should guilt-trip you into doing what he did. He girded up his loins and knocked on stranger's doors to open himself to the mercy of their response to his Invitation of the Gospel of Truth! Mike got his hands dirty helping the neighbors with marital problems, and he even prayed for them! All he had to do was share his story about how loving Jesus made his marriage all it could be. Neighboring for Jesus truly is the answer to world peace!

8

The Art of Taking

Have you ever been a crazy stalker who wants to totally give everything for the odd hope your special project will one day turn to you in total understanding that they are the princess to your king? Some relationships are like that: people give, give, give. While we might be justifying our actions by saying this person really needs help, the reality is we wallow in our own self-misery, wanting to feel better by 'helping' someone else! At first the target of our affection was flattered about attention, but eventually they grew as tired of us as we grew weary of giving everything to them, particularly when they were not reciprocating. The moral of the story here is we need to learn to receive just as much as we learn to give while still being neighborly. This is important because more neighborhoods are built on two-way streets, and so that is how the relationships are supposed to work.

Everyone likes to bring all their skills to the table so we can one-up everyone else in the room. Most of us want to prove our neighborly strength so we dress as Super Neighbor and refuse the help of anyone else. In our minds, we are perfect souls living in a twisted world, so it becomes our imperative to save the neighborhood. After all, if we refuse to let our neighbors help us in our needs, we limit what God can do in our neighborhood.

"To" and "From"

Gary and Kim live in perfect middle-class suburbia next to Helen, a single mother. They always considered Helen their personal project for Jesus. Gary was always mowing her lawn and shoveling her driveway while Kim baked her cookies and listened to her problems. One day Gary was spreading mulch around the garden when he came up a bag short. Helen happened to have extra mulch and totally wanted Gary and Kim to have it, but our perfect couple was just too perfect to admit any need, even one as trivial as one more bag of mulch. They wanted to give *to* Helen, but never wanted to get *from* her.

Helen insisted they accept the mulch so intently her eyes glowed red while declaring in a voice that could only come from the Devil, "You will take my mulch!" Such a supernatural display of evil snapped Gary and Kim out of their stubbornness. The couple talked about it later and realized they were always giving to Helen, but never letting Helen meet any of their needs. The act of receiving the mulch gave Helen a boost of self-esteem and we all know feeling good about ourselves is the key to true happiness in life.

The principle is rather clear: when we are too focused on giving but never open up to getting anything from our neighbors, we rob needy people of their dignity making them dependent on our generosity. On the contrary, when we are open to receiving from neighbors, everyone's self esteem gets built up, and we all know Jesus came to make our psyches feel good.

Admit You Are Needy

Being a good neighbor is learning to both give and receive. Such interplay strikes our pride, and us American Christians cling to our pride as Sméagol is drawn to the One Ring. This means admitting we are needy becomes a challenge but it is important to make our neighbors feel good about themselves.

I am not a handyman and if I attempt to build something it tends to crumble like a house of cards, and thus my wife becomes really nervous when I go near tools even for simple things like fixing the death trap of our garage steps. My wife had created a 'honey do' list that was posted on the wall of my man cave and I dreaded those handyman projects because each failed attempt would pierce my soul as my manhood was subject to question at my failed handyman projects.

After six months of procrastinating the repairs to the garage steps I was being a good neighbor by hanging out in Roger's man cave which doubled as his garage. I looked over and saw the most elegant steps I have ever seen in my life. An angel sat upon them while a heavenly spotlight shone on the stairs from above. I asked about the heavenly decent of Jacob's Ladder and he said, "Oh, yeah, I threw those together one boring afternoon." Immediately I thought this would be a good way for me to test out my ability to demonstrate how needy I can be in the handyman department so I asked him to look at the death trap in my garage.

That glorious day my neighbor took only thirty minutes fixing the step my wife has been nagging me about for over six months. I handed him tools, got us beverages, and let him work his skill to fill one of my needs! It was awesome. My neighbor felt so good about himself and my wife stopped nagging me about the steps! That is the art of taking in full action.

Just Force It

We need to remember our motives when we are looking for places to get things from our neighbors. We can't force the relationship by always going over and asking for sugar because they will start to think we really need help managing our pantry, but if we are in the middle of baking cookies and did not count the cost, by all means we should ask for a little sugar. Just remember, do not go looking for something to get, but let your getting flow from the natural course of life. This way we will not be compromising our integrity by asking for something we really do not need.

I believe borrowing things from our neighbors has become a lost art in America. Borrowing something from next door is not only a sign of ill-preparedness, but also weakness...not to mention the neighbor creeps us out and he might just give us rat poisoning instead of sugar! But I believe when we are in genuine need we should learn to ask our neighbor for help because it will help to forge the relationship, and better relationships lead to opportunities to tell others about how much we love Jesus!

An Act of Scriptural Twisting

Because this is supposed to be a Christian book we have to throw in a Bible verse every chapter to make it seem like this thing is supported by Jesus. Even though the Bible is full of awesome principles like bearing one another's burdens, being part of a community, or any number of equality qualifying verses that might actually support what we are trying to say here, we will instead focus on a totally mistranslated verse and we will even cram in some pop psychology! Here it goes:

Somewhere in Luke, probably chapter 7 is this story of a party (after all, Jesus parties a lot). At this party a woman who was known around town as a prostitute was pouring expensive oil all over Jesus's feet and then washing it off with oil. During this weird scene, Jesus and this woman were made very vulnerable because there were important religious men in attendance. Jesus could not reject this strange offering because it would have emotionally crippled the prostitute. While it was probably true Jesus did not need a foot washing, that is all this woman had to offer and he received it willingly because his receiving of the gift meant everything to this woman, and Jesus is too kind to hurt her little psyche. By accepting the gift, Jesus was giving her dignity!

The point is Jesus made himself vulnerable to receive such a weird gift from such a great sinner. In short, he is willing to receive from us, so Jesus, too, practiced the art of taking!

9

The Art of Lacking Boundaries

oundaries is now a trending word in Christian circles thanks to a theologically devoid 'Christian' book on the subject. This chapter discusses how lacking boundaries starts innocently enough, but then we will have to put our foot down and become a jerk to bring balance back to our life. As an example consider Kevin and Richard. They became instant Backyard Buddies after Richard's wife baked cookies for Kevin's family. Life was going awesome while the women slaved in the kitchen, cooking and baking cookies and the men sat in the family room watching sports on television.

One fateful evening everything changed. Kevin knocked on the door telling stories of a frying-pan battle he just had with his wife. He needed a place to stay the night so his wife did not go all Lorena Bobbit on him in the night. Richard could not turn Kevin down after all those cookies and football games, so of course he let Kevin sleep on the couch. Before

Richard knew it, Kevin was sleeping on his couch all week, not talking to his wife, and just becoming a roomie to Richard's family.

I know what you are thinking, "Why give Kevin a room in the basement when he needs encouragement to talk to his wife, and maybe a marriage counselor's phone number?" Simple: Christians are supposed to be doormats who just do everything for everyone who ever asks, because that is how God answers prayer, at least that's the way he should do it!

Causing the Mess

When we start taking the Great Commandment seriously, we become involved with the riffraff on the block. Like anyone else who does not love Jesus their lives will be total shambles until such a time as they profess to love him. In the mean time, God has put us on the block to be responsible for helping fill the needs that come bubbling to the surface like scum on a stagnant pond. Of course, it is bad enough these heathens lives are horrible, but often times we find ourselves not helping the situation, but making it worse because we end up giving our neighbors something they clearly need, but they should be getting on their own. Lets look at some scenarios:

Chaotic Crisis

When we first become backyard buddies with someone, our new friend looks perfect, just like we are and we assume they probably already love Jesus but have not yet told us as much. After a while we find they are actually very rotten people. The surface of their lives is polished like white-washed tombs but underneath they yell at each other, smack puppies, and their children are not obedient! Once we find these dirty little secrets laying in the house beside ours we start to feel like it is our responsibility to step in. At that point, we have made the situation worse.

Attention-Starvation

Some people just want attention. We all know the type: we are always praying they are not in the front yard when we walk the dog because of the conversation we are drawn into like light being pulled into a black hole. These people are totally starved for attention and because we love Jesus, we are required to talk to them for as long as they want, anything less is just not Christian! This person is particularly troubling because of how close they live to us. The combination of our proximity and our wondrous charm lends itself to become embroiled in conversations even at times when we walk the dog the other way! Once we are sucked into this relationship, there is no escape except pure rudeness, but such an action might prevent this person from ever loving Jesus!

Co-Dependence

Even worse than the attention starved person is the emotionally needy person who can only turn to us in times of emotional distress. These people do not have family, other friends, and their co-workers do not live on the block. They are heathens who do not attend church, and because we are supposed to love Jesus and take the Great Commandment seriously we are the person it falls to in order to give them support. The problem is they are perpetually needy! Once we embrace help-ing them, it would be rude to stop, after all, the ultimate goal is to get them to profess to love Jesus and they certainly will not do that if we ever push them away!

When our neighbors find out we are Christians they will often walk all over us like a doormat and it is rude to turn them away. But if they are not praying to profess their love in Jesus, we may have no alternative but to set some boundaries, and hopefully, despite our rudeness, maybe we can muster a profession from them in the long run anyway.

Responsibility To and For

Boundaries are like yards and everyone should respect the boundary markers, but our radical world lacking parental teaching, general coarseness, and the fact that so many people fail to love Jesus means no one can tell whose yard is whose. This leads to teenage hoodlums next door driving all over our otherwise perfectly manicured lawn. But even worse is when we do not respect one another's personal space, and that space is called boundaries.

The best place to learn about boundaries is another book of that approximate title[2]. The psychology in that book is great, but the theology is as bankrupt as this book, so if you like this book, you will love that one! In that book they define boundaries as the place separating me from you. This means knowing what I can do and what I can't do for my neighbor. In other words, we need to look at our responsibility. As people who love Jesus and are taking the Great Commandment seri-ously we are *responsible to* help our neighbors. But our teach-ing on this topic may well have swung the pendulum too far and now we think we are *responsible for* our neighbors. These little, tiny words *to* and *for* have big meaning. The difference being *responsibility to* our neighbors means we have to do all manner of service, prayer, and anything else it takes to get them to pray a little prayer that starts them on their path of loving Jesus. But it does not mean we are responsible for how they react to us. Their own path of loving Jesus is all up to them. It does not matter if they are raging alcoholics or still flinging their children across the house...as long as they profess to love Jesus everything will be OK in the end!

Recently my friend Ken told me about a story that was so providential I knew I had to include it in this book. Ken became friends with the college-age neighbor, but this kid ruined his life by not going to college, choosing instead to became a weed-smoking punk without a job or a car.

This kid came up to Ken and started asking for help. Most people, particularly after reading this far into our plan would feel totally guilty for our personal success and we should become convinced the best thing to do is to write a check to buy the kid a car. After all, if you truly love your neighbor you should just give him whatever his felt needs are! While there are times this approach could be the right course of action, this time it would have been giving the kid too much opportunity to blow the cash on a brick of weed. Instead, Ken decided to sell his ugly old car to the kids mother so he could pawn off the problem on her to deal with. That is keeping boundaries!

Of course, like every story in this book, the kid turned his life around because Ken loved Jesus and was being a good neighbor.

Hands and Handouts

The concept of *to* and *for* extends to giving someone a hand and giving them a handout. We will not spend any time talking about the difference between those two concepts, but I will explain it with horrible exposition of a biblical story that could only come from the book of Luke. In fact, we already twisted this story one way, now we will wring it another!

The Good Samaritan is a story about boundaries. This nice Samaritan picked up the man whom was rejected by the religious leaders. Back at the inn, (or was that a hospital?) we see the Samaritan did not cancel all of his plans like a good Christian might do (apart from reading this chapter). This poor beaten and robbed man was in need, so the Samaritan should have canceled his trip and stayed with the man to nurse him back to health! Is that not what we all should have done in this terrible situation? I mean really, if that did not cross your mind as being the right thing to do, you should be ashamed of yourself! I know I might be projecting the antithesis of this chapter on you right now, but I need to make the point that is wrong! The Good Samaritan was a story in the Bible about boundaries, how to teach us that we should help (preferably our neighbor) but then get back on with our life! Failure to do this crosses the line from giving a man a hand to giving him a handout, and we all know that the Republicans hate handouts, so we need to avoid those or else we might be accused of being a democrat!

This reminds me of a story about my neighbor. The poor man lost his job, his savings was gone, and he was crying to us that he might lose his house. He was dropping every hint in the book that he needed money but he was too afraid to come right out and ask. Just like any good Christian who loves Jesus, we wanted to write the guy a check, but we remembered we are republicans and handouts are bad, so we took the higher road and made a lot of calls looking for people who might be able to hire an out-of-work trucker. We spent time making calls to assemble a list of potential employers, but the man never called anyone on the list. If we simply gave him money, he would need more next month, so we opted to help him find a job. Sadly the guy never called anyone on our list, but because we love Jesus, everything worked out anyway! He got another job and we are still friends.

In the end it was better to help him find a job than it was to give him money. I know, however, some of you think we should have done more. We should have given the guy money or made the calls for him, but you are wrong! We should not give handouts, that would make us look like democrats!

Loving to Call

Did you know that Jesus set boundaries? He helped some people but not others. Sometimes he was with the crowds but other times he left them behind. Some people were cured but not everyone...these were all very clear teachings from Jesus about setting boundaries. I do not have any verses to back this up, but I am a pastor, so trust me!

The reality of the matter is once we start becoming friends with our neighbors they will love to call, and the distractions are always a welcome way to stop doing those boring, monotonous things we all need to do. When we start setting boundaries we wonder if we are pushing the neighbor away too fast or if we should do more in their time of need.

Sometimes when we do not push them away we wonder if we are doing too much! How do I find balance in all these boundaries? Do not worry about it, just embrace these words of Jesus: "This *is* the best way to live. When we love God and love our neighbors, we are living the way Jesus intends for us.[3]" Yes, indeed, loving neighbors is such a messy job we wonder if we were right to start embracing these concepts.

We had a difficult situation with our neighbor and her teenage daughter. This girl was of driving age but did not have a car. She liked to stay up late often causing her to miss the bus for school. The first couple times she asked my wife for a ride to school it was not a problem but soon it happened my wife was giving her a ride to school a few times per week, so we decided to be cruel and put an end to that. We first offered our help to find her a job so she could buy her own car but she failed to send out the job applications we picked up from Chick-fil-A and Hobby Lobby. Once she stopped receiving our help finding a job, we had to tell them we could no longer offer rides.

This choice was hard to make at the time but we think we were right. This is the type of boundary Jesus wants us to set. While we could give more money or more time, we can't do everything. The reality of being a good neighbor is it often times takes some prayer to figure out how to set those boundaries. At least we can join a charismatic church so we can hear from God a whole lot more than those other churches who deny God still speaks with us!

10

The Art of Laser Focus

It is imperative we learn with whom in our life we can share a good relationship. We only have twenty four hours a day, so we should all seriously consider quitting our jobs to become full-time good neighbors, but for those who need income to pay bills, we can instead learn to focus like a laser instead. We found for some reason not everyone will be as enthused about being a good neighbor as we are. We have no idea why because as Christians we all know the importance of being connected; the question is how we convey that importance onto the neighbors who do not yet profess to love Jesus.

As we start neighboring, we find many whom do not share our interest in 'connecting'. We will examine some of their excuses, but I need to stress that not everyone will become backyard buddies. Some folks will want a good, deep relationship with their neighbors while others merely gaze with an evil countenance when we try to hand them an Invitation of the Gospel of Truth. Some will even chase us off with a broom! We need to learn to spend time only with people who actually want a relationship.

Some Reasons People Don't Care

Some people just do not care about this neighboring stuff and others do not have an interest in us as people! If folks do not seem enthusiastic when approached about having a block party, we may need to assume on some level, they just do not care. Here are some reasons we find people do not care about this neighboring stuff:

- *Too Busy.* Yes, it is true many people perceive their life as fulfilling without the need to participate in a Block Party of Salvation. They may have full time jobs, hobby groups, and online social gatherings lending to a happy life, hence, they have little desire to meet all the crazy neighbors whom could potentially be a drain on their personal space. If only they would realize that Jesus commanded us to be a good literal neighbor we might convince them to help with the block party.
- *Wary of Us.* It is hard to believe but some people just think we are crazy. They are not fearful or anything, they just believe Jesus freaks who want to throw block parties have an ~~ulterior~~ ultimate motive.
- *Relationally Full Tank.* Some people are really not sitting at home crying because they were not invited to the neighbor's house because most people actually have a great circle of friends. Sure, they will gladly

lend you a tool or a cup of sugar, but they do not feel anything missing from their life because of the circle of friends they do have! Such people are also deluded, but they have no felt needs, so let them be for now.

- *Different Phases, Different Stages.* Some people already paid their family dues and do not want to be surrounded by a plethora of screaming neighborhood brats at dinner or a block party. These folks might be in a totally different stage of life as us and are not really looking for anything more.

- *Secrets to Keep.* Some people have deep, dark secrets. Secretive people are likely ax murderers or bank robbers afraid of exposure. They might say the wrong thing and let slip their horrible life secrets. Perhaps they are afraid of being recognized as the guy in a police sketch. Still others are child flingers or have bad marriages and do not want the whole neighborhood to know about it. These people are just strange, after all, who does not like friends and block parties?

Twisting Jesus to Make a Point

When we throw block parties of salvation we will become enamored with crowds of people like Jesus. It will become difficult to figure out how to best spend our time, so when that happens, we must look at the WWJD bracelet on our wrist and ask, "What Would Jesus Do?" Then we can maybe remember that Jesus was surrounded by crowds often, but he practiced the skill of laser focusing.

First we read somewhere in Luke 10 how Jesus selected only 72 people from the hordes of hungry zombies surrounding him for a very special mission, but he went even further in identifying 12 apostles who were able to hear his teachings clearly. But in Matthew 17:1-9 and Mark 14:32-42 we see that from the of group of 12 he selected only three disciples to accompany him on special occasions.

So that WWJD bracelet will help us become laser focused. We need to start by throwing the Block Party of Salvation to become the neighborhood hero and draw a huge crowd. From the huge crowds, we select a small group of people to join us for a private dinner, sort of like an interview process. Of those friends who seem to be the best neighbors we need to pick three, because that is God's number. Those three will become the people we focus on. Do this and we will be just like Jesus!

A Person of Parties

We need to keep kingdom-focused while we engage in neighborhood relational building, so we should select an ally from among our neighbors. Find the guy who is good at throwing parties; this is just what Jesus told the 72 people he sent out in pairs. He clearly says to go into these towns and stay with people who are really good at throwing parties. Jesus wanted the disciples to stay with these families because they would introduce the disciples to their friends and this would have the greatest kingdom impact leading way more people into a shallow profession of loving Jesus.

The phrase in the Bible is 'Person of Peace' which clearly means someone who is open to visitors. Rather than commanding the disciples to move around, Jesus knew the Person of Peace would have large social networks, most likely consisting of their neighbors in the eight closest houses, all properly friended on Facebook. In other words, Jesus was directing his disciples to stay at the houses of the towns very best neighbors! He was such a genius.

This Bible passage tells us exactly who we need to choose as our neighborly ally: The guy who is better at throwing wild parties than we are. Ask God to direct you to this person. The signs of such a party animal are pretty clear. First, look for the house with piles of cars in front of it several times a week. You do need to pray it is not a gathering of Amway sales people, but it might be worth that chance. Also, people who have lots of holiday decorations are a logical choice; these people usually have tons of people over during special events. Take a walk on Super Bowl Sunday and see who might be throwing a pigskin get-together, those people know how to party! They already have a desire to connect, but it is up to you to give them the vision to connect with the neighborhood.

This type of thing happened on my block. My church was delivering these sermons on being a good neighbor and I was starting to feel guilty because I was not throwing block parties. One day it occurred to me the neighbor always gathered tons of people into his garage and became noisy. I was starting to feel dejected because I was never invited over there where lots of people were clearly having fun. This guy was truly the Person of Parties and I knew he was the ally I have been searching for.

I decided to do something radical: Crash the party. Even though I was not invited I entered the garage where the strangers gathered. I was awe-struck to find this neighbor setup the garage as the ultimate party zone. Within moments I saw a karaoke bar, a liquor bar, and even a keg, complete with a naked drunk guy, a lampshade on his head, dancing away upon the keg! Suddenly it occurred to me my measly little garage full of worldly junk was not the best place for the block party, but this guy was just hosting parties of the people he knew which did not seem to include anyone on the block.

I confronted him about his great gift for parties and suggested he should throw one of those wild parties for the neighbors. I left out that whole Jesus motivation because I thought it might not go well with the bar and kegs, but I knew I had the ability to sneak Jesus in just like I had crashed the party myself. It did not take much convincing. The neighbor caught the vision for the block party like a bad cold and we went all out!

We hired a band, doubled up on the quantities of liquor, and invited all the neighbors. It was such a wild bash even the cops showed up, but since all the neighbors were getting wasted at our Block Party of Salvation, there were no complaints. This is truly the place for Jesus to become known, and much to my surprise, because we love Jesus so much our neighbors even decided to host a Bible study! The point is very clear. If you focus on the person of parties, you will gather huge crowds and be able to get on with your ~~ulterior~~ ultimate motive of getting tons of people to make a shallow profession of love for Jesus!

Foolish Investing

Sometimes we need to realize our neighbors are not interested in our desire to connect the neighborhood. When my wife and I first moved into town we noticed the older couple next door.

I began seeing visions of the elderly couple being like grand-parents to my kids. They were a really nice older couple and we think our kids are the best children in the world so what could possibly be wrong with getting all these people together. We found that we invited this elderly couple over several times but they kept rejecting our offer. My dreams of bringing these old people so close to the end of their life to make a profession of love for Jesus were being dashed as were my goals of having foster grandparents living right next door. Regardless, I kept asking them to come over until one day the husband calmly said, "Tom, I have paid my dues with little children. We really do not want kids around us during this stage of our life! Please, I know you are being nice, but with our bridge club and everything else we are doing in our sunset years, we just do not have any interest in this 'neighboring' gibberish you keep babbling about." I realized then I was investing my time foolishly. Good focus means I need to find another neighbor to bother.

After gramps gave me the cold shoulder I was sulking in the back yard when from over the fence I heard someone outside playing with kids who sounded about the age of my children, so I thought this was totally perfect. The man introduced himself as Mr. Smith, and I invited the family over for dinner. Things seemed to be going great. I would invite them over and they always seemed willing to visit, but my wife noticed they never invited us to anything. Our relationship was very one directional, we did all the inviting, so one day my wife suggested we merely stop asking them over. They never really seemed to care about the cold shoulder we gave them, so that told us it was foolish to waste all this time on neighbors who were not actively participating in creating neighborhood relationships.

Ultimately, neither of these relationships went anywhere. Do not let that crush your fragile psyche and definitely do not think our perfect plan in this book is wrong, you just need to learn to focus like a laser by spending your time with neighbors who are responsive and open to neighborly relationships. God will bring you to a neighbor who will catch your vision so you will have a partner in saving the block. You just need more faith.

Why Aren't We Being Discerning

After I got over licking my wounds inflicted by the Smiths never returning our friendly advancements I decided I would hang out in random neighbor's driveways. Invariably they would always come down and ask why I was there, so I told them about my vision for our neighborhood and how we could usher in world peace right here. Many of them just wrote me off as the neighborhood weirdo, but eventually one couple caught my vision like the flu and we became excellent neighbors. We shared meals, they shared meals with us, and then one weekend we all went camping. Finally we had neighbors who seemed like they wanted a relationship with us as much as we wanted one with them.

This couple taught us why we were not being discerning before. In the past with the elderly couple and the Smiths we were working too hard to be friends, but true friendships flow naturally. We were not being discerning with our relational time in the past because we were working too hard to make this neighboring stuff work rather than looking at the end of each driveway for a person who did not think us weird. We have to learn to invest our neighboring time mostly with those people who want a relationship. Once we find that couple, we can throw a block party to slowly reel in more folks to start a shallow relationship with Jesus.

The strategy is easy. We need to ask ourselves which families on the block connect well. We want couples who will embrace our buzz words and connect relationally to realize a maximum kingdom impact. Always remember your ~~ulterior~~ ultimate motive. Be friendly with everyone, but close to only a few. Then you will be just like Jesus.

11

The Art of Excusing

lock Parties of Salvation lead to perfect utopia in our neighborhoods. When this occurs, everyone becomes one with all things, but the reality is people often do not get along. Peter moved on the block and had immediate problems with his new neighbor because of a yapping chihuahua. The taco-peddling creature was a total yapfest, constantly barking and no one at the neighbor's house seemed to care.

Peter thought about his options. His first thought was poison, but then he thought that too obvious, he would likely be caught, and that would hinder his motive of getting these people to pray to love Jesus. Even a call to the police was a little out of order because it might have been too obvious it was the new guy on the block, so he decided a note would be better.

Peter spilled his heart onto paper about the horrible experience he encountered because of Ren, the Dog. He hoped the neighbor would become instantly sorry he ever bought that taco-chowing pooch. Peter included a phone number to talk over the matter and hopefully reduce the dog to silence. Sadly nothing ever changed, probably because it was a windy day and the note blew away. Peter went over there in a mad tirade screaming about why the neighbor did not read the letter or do anything about the dog. The neighbor became defensive because he did not know what Peter was talking about, so Peter kept yelling about the note. They could not even come to the issue about the dog and the matter was left unresolved. Peter knew he should be a good neighbor because this guy clearly did not love Jesus and he had to the be the one to save him, he just did not know what to do in this situation because he had left his WWJD bracelet at home.

My Neighbors are my Mortal Foes

We all live on blocks where there are people who do not love Jesus and such people cause all manner of problems. While some neighbors become our backyard buddies, others become mortal foes because they are rotten to the core and they repeatedly fling around children while letting the dog bark. Conflict with such neighbors is expected because we all have disagreements and our current world focuses on ourselves and our perfect little psyches and that means we perceive everyone else as being in the wrong. It is so bad that petty little things like unmowed lawns and loud music cause neighborhood bickering culminating in all out war. Things could get so bad that the neighbor might bulldoze your house! Don't let things go that far because you will lose all ability to get that neighbor to pray to love Jesus.

Of course when things go bad on the block we have some options. The first thing is to totally ignore the neighbor. Just like the little cut on our finger left untreated with antibiotics, ignoring the neighbor will result in an infected and festering neighborhood wound ending in feuds that are flat out comical to all the other neighbors who actually get along.

The real solution once again brings us back to Luke 10. The Great Commandment clearly demonstrates we are to love our literal neighbors (not everyone else out there – that is too broad). The Bible even says that loving your literal neighbors is the true key to good living! Do this and perfect utopia will break out on the block! This means we need to heal those broken neighborhood relationships.

First we need to determine the level of problem. Some things are completely inconsequential so we need to become more of a Christian doormat boldly proclaiming "WWJD" while letting the dogs bark and the music blare. We need to give the neighbors copious amounts of grace because there is clearly nothing that can be done about the noise they produce. Other problems, however, are more important. A drug dealer might live next door attracting shady gang-bangers who zoom up and down the street at all hours. This type of situation needs to be resolved quickly because they are a threat to the perfect image of the block, so a call to the authorities is the best solution. Just count that one as a soul lost to the fire!

Well, Excuuuuseee me

Many problems in our neighborhoods relate to people subtly poking our little bubble of total perfection. "It would be so peaceful around here if that dog would just stop barking" we tell ourselves. The majority of our concerns are just people living their life around us but their mere presence disturbs our perfect silence. We do not want to hear any music unless it is our stereo playing, and our lawn must remain perfect unless we are the ones walking on it. In truth, we are self-centered and easily annoyed.

It is easy to downplay these concerns and force a fake Christian smile, but sometimes things really do need to be addressed in the neighborhood and we try to put on the fake smile about those things, too. When something is truly wrong, however, we need to learn to ignore the offense. Now, we do not use the word *ignore* because that is too passive. Instead we will use the term *forgive* because that is more 'Christian'. We are really just doing the same thing. We are ignoring the constant offense because we realize how much we have been forgiven. We do not need to confront the neighbor. A good neighbor should just forget how loud the music plays or that the dog is constantly barking.

Some problems are larger, such as, when the neighborhood kids keep playing hide and seek in the garden or their dog keeps getting out and pooping on the lawn. Those cases require a conversation with the neighbor to resolve, and if there is a drug dealer in the hood pullin' yo' property Benjamins down then the police should haul that guy away. Regardless of the big or small offense we need to let it go whether it has been resolved or not, that is what Jesus would do.

Forgetting and Reconciling

Sometimes we need to forget about what our neighbor has done, but that does not mean you need to become the guy's backyard buddy. When a neighbor is constantly invading our perfect bubble it may be easy to harbor hatred, but remember Jesus said to let it go. We are letting go the anger, the desire to get back at the neighbor, or the desire to call the police on him. But the command from Jesus says nothing about being a friend, so you can go on just not being the guy's friend. This is the difference between forgetting and reconciling. If we are forgetting about it, we do not harbor the hatred, but if we reconcile we are allowing the relationship to continue.

Let's get theological for a moment. God offers forgiveness to everyone...or is it just the elect...no, that is too evil of God, it is everyone. Whether or not we receive forgiveness is a different matter all together. Theologically, we are clearly all forgiven, so we will be in heaven, right? But only those of us who take that forgiveness will fall in love with Jesus, and that is when we have a relationship with him. This means that everyone is offered forgiveness, so God does not harbor the hatred, but only some of us are reconciled to become God's backyard buddies!

Just like with God, we need to first offer forgiveness to the neighbors. If we are trying to become friends with the guy without forgiving his yapping chihuahua, we will find our relationship cannot move on. Reconciliation, however, allows us to keep being friends after we have offered forgiveness, but only if the guy takes the forgiveness. Reconciliation also contains boundaries about what the person can do. It makes sure we can be friends, but if the neighbor is a child flinger we cannot trust them to babysit the kids, and if they have a dog, it must be quiet!

Forgetting about our neighbor's transgressions cannot be a matter of the mind or logical thought, but rather, a matter of heart. This makes forgetting easier because we ignore facts and let the neighbor walk all over us like the doormats we Christians are supposed to be. We need to bless the neighbors who curse us, this will make them feel bad unless they are YouTube stars or were featured on Jersey Shore. Jesus will allow us to forget perfectly, so do just that.

The Miracle of Memory Loss

Peter (not the apostle, but the guy from the opening story) decided to forget about the yapping chihuahua and *heap burning coals upon the neighbor's head*. It was a horribly snowy day so Peter shoveled the neighbor's driveway. A man came out of the house and thanked Peter for shoveling. It was the neighbor's brother. The man explained his brother was diagnosed with cancer. Suddenly Peter felt like a jerk for complaining about a barking dog during such a horrible time in the neighbor's life. Suddenly Peter's family knew they had a ministry of serving up meals, lawn work, and babysitting. This forged a real friendship between the two houses. Does that chihuahua still yap it's head off? Peter said, "I don't know. I forgot about it just like I forgot about all my unresolved attempts to get the thing to stop yapping."

This fantastic story illustrates that every time you experience a neighborhood annoyance and it goes unresolved it is because that house is experiencing tragedy and you have just identified your ministry. You should immediately look to do something such as mow the lawn or shovel the driveway. This will always let you know what the family is struggling through and provide an opportunity to serve them until you are backyard buddies. All you need to do is take the Great Commandment seriously and love your literal neighbors like Jesus said to do.

When neighborhood struggles arise we often want to just forget about it and move on but Jesus wants us to do more. He wants to use that struggle with the neighbor to transform us into the person God wants us to be and that is the genius behind the Great Commandment. Here are some steps to consider when neighborhood problems arise.

- *Identify the issue and assess who is at fault.* Beginning from a posture of self-centeredness realize we, as the Christians, are likely never the one at fault, after all, we love Jesus and the neighbor does not, but we might need to forget about that to bring the neighbor to a profession of love for Jesus.

- *Choose to obey Jesus in praying for enemies on the block.* Pray for the neighbor who is the mortal enemy of the universe and also pray God might make them come to the light and profess to love Jesus.

- *When convicted of wrongdoing, look for an immediate way to justify our actions in our mind.* We love Jesus and so we are perfect and in the right, so embrace any potential conviction as clearly not a problem with us. Do what it takes to lay conviction to rest in our mind.

- *Be Extra Annoying.* Everyone wants to be served, even those people who are annoying, so make sure to look for every possible way to do something for them which they should be doing for themselves. Always ask what is the most loving way to annoy the neighbor today?

- *Become Secret Santa to the neighborhood.* Some neighbors are so hard-hearted they do not respond to direct acts of kindness, so we must be sneaky with our service. This usually requires going out at 3:00 AM to quietly rake leaves, but this allows us to do good things without having to meet the old miser next door.

In modern America, we do not suffer any real persecution so God wants to use the challenges in our neighborhoods to shape us into what we should become. We grow in Christ by suffering through neighborhood conflicts because our perfect lives are just too cushy. Embrace the conflict and know for sure that the barking chihuahua is your cross to carry.

12

Better Listening to God

God wants us to use the principles in this book to usher peace into the world one neighborhood at a time. Some musician once posted music to the internet and asked people to perform their own song on YouTube with the music so he could steal it to compose a single song. The publicity stunt worked and he even went on to give a TED talk! What began with one person spread to hundreds of others around the world resulting in a masterpiece. When one person makes the music it is nothing special, but if everyone does their part, something bigger happens.

The big picture concept is part of being a neighborhood, but it all starts with listening to God about the Great Commandment. Alone we can't do anything, but teaming up with our party-hardy neighbor to organize a Block Party of Salvation can introduce the neighbors to each other. But what would happen if the neighbors learned to live in perfect unity?

Those neighborhoods could literally usher world peace into a city creating perfect unity. Cities would join cities, countries would learn to get along with other countries, then Iraqis and Israelites would start holding hands and singing *Kumbaya*. But this will not happen if *you* do not obey God in throwing a block party.

Our group of pastors came to the conclusion this neighboring thing could be big when we sat in my living room dreaming a big, hairy, audacious dream about world peace. We came to the conclusion God wanted us to put together another gimmicky church program, toss in relevant trendy words, and hire a marketing team so we could once and for all build our churches and solve the world's problems. We understood it would be hard. While we often want to just close that garage door at night, obeying Jesus's command to loving the people in the eight closest houses to ours forces us to obey to God.

A Big, Hairy, Audacious Dream

When pastors from shallow churches gather around to talk about 'kingdom causes' oftentimes silliness ensues. In our case we gathered together twenty pastors and brought in the best Christian speaker we could muster: the city manager. This guy told us about all the problems burdening the city and merely declared to us if all the bodies warming chairs in our churches would just look out for the their neighbors, many of the challenges in our city would be resolved. As a collective group of pastors, we decided to write one sermon series around the twisted, narrow perspective that Jesus meant the eight closest houses to us when he told us to love our neighbors (anything more than that is just too nebulous).

We collectively preached this twisted plan to eight thousand households. I am not good at math, but if eight thousand households each told eight neighbors about this stuff that could be 64,000 households overnight! All this could be done if everyone obeyed God in creating a tic-tac-toe grid and organized a Block Party of Salvation. Our plan was a success and within a few years we had a cult-like following of people who forgot everything about sound biblical teaching and were merely focused on throwing block parties and preaching the gospel about how block parties will usher in world peace.

This thing is growing out of control! Shallow pastors around the country are hearing of this thing and letting their congregations know the ministry God wants everyone around this country to do. They are teaching their congregations to set aside the pesky calling their congregants have discerned from God and follow the church's plan instead...after all, it has been centuries since the crusades and following the mission of the church is safe now!

Our efforts encouraged people all around the world hearing these messages to become a works-based group of neighboring fanatics. Our commitment to the Great Commandment resulted in lawns being mowed, driveways getting shoveled, and neighbors all over our town made shallow commitments to love Jesus as a result of our Block Parties of Salvation. This just proves, Jesus was a genius!

The Jehovah's Witnesses and Mormons were Right

If you have ever been visited by Mormons or Jehovah's Witnesses you know they go out in teams. They are right! You will have a better chance neighboring when allied with another person, so share this book with your neighbors to see who catches the neighboring bug and wants to help organize the Block Party of Salvation.

To find your Shallow Neighbor counterpart, start by inviting one household over to listen to your idea. This person does not even need to be someone who loves Jesus, at least not the way we love Jesus. The neighborhood mystic, Buddhist, or Hindu might know far more about neighboring than we do, so they would make the perfect ally to team up with for the Block Party of Salvation. All truth is God's truth, so find anyone whom is able to start conversations with random strangers because God will honor the actions of anyone trying to be a good neighbor, after all, it aligns with his ultimate purposes of bringing the neighbors together through a block party. Don't talk yourself into thinking you are too busy to get started, just find the guy who is better at talking to people than you and the two of you can start planning the block party.

Don't forget we all have gifts given to us by God to help throw the block party. If we have tried to be a good neighbor in the past and have not had any luck than it is possible our gifts are not in knocking on doors to pass out Invitations of the Gospel of Truth. Not everyone is naturally social, but we know that goes against the clear teachings of Jesus, so what are we to do? Very simple: pawn off the invitations to neighborhood Hindu while we tackle the food details.

Perhaps you are the socialite in the neighborhood and really want to bring everyone together so you want to organize everything but details just are not your thing. You could invite all the people and let the social deviant on the block work out the details; he will not be distracted by people anyway. The point is, everyone needs to stay in their gifts. While one person may be very talented at talking to people, another may have been blessed with the spiritual gift of manning the grill. Figure out your role in the block party and serve there. Once everyone does their part in the party, world peace is sure to break out and people will pray to love Jesus in droves.

When enough shallow pastors rise to influence in any given town, multiple churches may conspire together to preach our series of emotionally manipulative sermons to get their congregations to give up their clear calling and devote their life to neighboring. When these coalitions happen, awesome things occur on the block. One story related to me had three different churches represented on one block, and all three churches were preaching on neighboring! This lead to awesome discussions strong-arming the other neighbors, but a problem was quickly realized: whose church do all these neighborhood heathens attend? The block party committee decided to table that challenge to focus instead on a neighborhood movie night. They decided to break the law by assembling a huge outdoor screen and displaying movies for all of the neighbors to come and watch. Of course they opened with a prayer that some DMCA lawyer would not drive by, and God protected this group.

Eventually the group moved beyond mere movie nights and began including a pot luck dinner. Clearly there was a Baptist church among those represented. The bottom line is great conversations ensued because multiple churches preached about neighboring thus sparking a group of people to illegally display movies and have potlucks. My friends recounting the story even told me they were starting to include movies that have a Christian message like *The Shack* and *Exodus*! This would usher shallow neighborhood professions of love for Jesus and an expansion of the wading-pool of faith among our neighbors. It is clear that partnering with a Mormon will expand the cause of Christ!

The Power of Working with a Hindu

Great things happen when neighbors catch a vision together. The Bible is full of stories about teams of people turning the world on its head by going to China. Twelve apostles made the world a better place by healing people and organizing others to feed widows. Luke reports that Jesus sends out disciples in twos to proclaim his coming, and Paul worked in a few different teams. God's story is told by teams of people who literally change the world.

Despite all these great results, people who love Jesus and the shallow churches they represent do not team up like we think they should. Partnerships to usher the whole world into utopic unity based on a profession of love for Jesus should be championed among churches everywhere. I think I have determined two reasons people are not joining with other believers in this perfect plan of neighborly love: Biblical Discernment and Concern Over Our Church Doctrine.

Biblical Discernment

While there are certainly some non-essentials in the Christian life such as music style, dress code, and Bible translation, a lot of methodologies many modern churches employ are not in alignment with the Bible. Often times when people do not feel comfortable with a focus on business models, and biblical misinterpretation makes some people very leery of teaming up with other people who merely profess Jesus. After all, those Mormons and Jehovah's Witnesses also carry Bibles and talk about God, but they do not believe the same things (at least that is what I have been told).

Taken together, some people may completely disagree with our scriptural analysis or our emphasis on modern business motivation buzzwords, and even though it is a great cause to be a good neighbor, our over-emphasis on neighboring may well be a turnoff for those who truly know Jesus, not just openly profess to love him.

Concern Over Church Doctrine

This goes hand in hand with biblical discernment. When a church in town has a reputation for twisting the Bible to get it's congregants to follow some crazy mission, some folks tend to get concerned. The crusades happened because church leaders put it into the people's head to go and kill for Jesus. The obvious difference is many people in that time period were not legally allowed to read the Bible, and it was not available in the common tongue. Today, we have extra Bibles, tons of translations, and legal, ready access to the Bible, but we just do not tend to read it and the churches do not encourage us to read it. So when someone does not buy into this stuff, he has probably figured out your church is likely one of these business motivation churches and rolls their eyes at the latest local

scheme to bring many people to a shallow profession of love for Jesus.

While some causes might be worth joining the same side, a framework based on such a sandy foundation is not one likely to have lasting impact and many people who do understand the Bible are more concerned with following the plan they have laid out directly with God rather than continuing on with a mission handed down to them by church leaders. We do not need another crusade!

Strange but Powerful

Jesus is a rocket scientist! He wanted us to be good neighbors because it really works! When everyone is a good neighbor, world peace breaks out one neighborhood at a time. When this happens on a city-sized scale all crime stops, people come together with a common chorus singing *Imagine* and wondering why the rest of the world is not as willing to set aside their differences and just love the person in the next house.

Just think of the possibilities for this life if every Christian misinterpreted what Jesus said about loving your neighbor as we have done in this book. What if we all just did what this book says, irregardless of what that big, hard to read Bible says and we all just loved the people who lived in the eight closest houses to us? What if we all just stopped doing the things God has called us to do in order to focus on having a barbecue with our best backyard buddies? What if we all stopped the things we were called to by God and instead all planned a Block Party of Salvation? There is so much potential here, we could easily change the world!

Pull out that tic-tac-toe board from chapter 2 and have a look at it. Look at how empty that is. You do not even know the names of the people in the eight houses closest to yours. You should be ashamed! You need to put aside all of the things God has shown, you and start working on filling in the names on that board. Starting today you need to become the neighborhood wacko knocking on everyone's door and getting their contact information. If they are not responsive, it calls for strange but radical approaches: dig through their garbage to gather the information they are not comfortable sharing with the neighborhood wacko.

Take walks in the neighborhood and stop to talk to everyone you see until you find one person who catches the idea of having a neighborhood block party. Look for that guy who can draw in a big crowd or put together a plan so powerful that even the devil will come to profess shallow love for Jesus! Commit to good neighboring and we will usher world peace and perfection onto this miserable planet!

Afterword

Beautiful Neighborhoods on Shifting Sand
An Apology

Y ou may read the word 'apology' and think I am sorry for this work or the things I have said, but like many other aspects of modern western Christianity, we have forgotten the meaning of *apology* which means *to give an answer*. Thus, when I write *An Apology*, I am not saying this was all in jest, but rather, I wish to now give a serious and sober response to *The Art of Neighboring* and how it will ultimately fail the Christian community in creating the lasting eternal impact on it's readers.

When my church decided to take time to preach some sermons about how we interact with our physical neighbors I watched closely as I always do. I take the command from Paul in 1 Thessalonians 5:21-22 very serious: *Examine everything carefully; hold fast to that which is good, abstain from every form of evil (NASB).* My church services are generally biblically sound, and to their credit, the pastoral staff did a good job of presenting this material in a manner that gave heed to scripture, but I remember leaning over to a friend at the start of the service on being a good neighbor and saying, "why are they not taking us to Luke 10:29?" Indeed, the staff did not go to the one passage that should have been the very cornerstone in a series on being a good neighbor. The man questioning Jesus asks, 'Who is my neighbor?' I kept going back waiting for the Sunday they would go to that one glaring passage in the Bible that seems to be missing, but it never came. To be honest, I am a busy person and I am not in the habit of being critical of sermons in church so I let it go until the local 'City Church' gathering.

What I did not know at the time is how many churches in our town were preaching the same sermon series. While I was cognizant of the book *The Art of Neighboring* and knew the pastors were using it as a framework, I determined it was probably not a book I would find value in reading. But when I saw how the book was being praised by this whole group of churches, and that the largest churches in my town were trying to start some 'neighboring movement' complete with commitment cards to organize block parties, I knew I needed to take a closer look. By happenstance I was dog-sitting for a friend whose church was also going through this neighboring series and she happened to have a copy of the book, so I purloined it to obtain the opportunity to read the tome. I was exactly correct in my gut instinct: This book is another example of modern-day theological garbage dotting the Christian landscape, promising yet another perfect plan to usher in a new awaking.

Once I saw yet another book promising to grow the community, grow the church, and save many people, I knew I could get mad, I could write a blog post, or I could just write a whole book and let the entire silliness of twenty-first century, first-world Christianity pour forth on the pages. While the twelve chapters preceding in this book represent a comical parody of *The Art of Neighboring* and modern Christian trends in general, the present chapter will take a serious tone as I detail what could possibly be so wrong with a book trying to help people know their neighbors better. Remember that not all things appearing Christian are really Christian, and even Jesus drove the money changers out of temple in righteous anger: *And Jesus entered the temple and drove out all those who were buying and selling in the temple, and overturned the tables of the money changers and the seats of those who were selling doves. And He said to them, "It is written, 'MY HOUSE SHALL BE CALLED A HOUSE OF PRAYER'; but you are making it a ROBBERS' DEN. (Matthew 21:12-13, NASB)"*

This chapter first details some points of praise for *The Art of Neighboring*, then we will look at some sociology, philosophy, psychology, and finally scripture. While I believe the scriptural analysis is enough for me to cast this book back to the swine, the other components could prove beneficial to people evaluating the soundness of future books promising through programs to give people a true taste of God. In reality, the way to truly know and grow close to Christ is through prayer and disciplined Bible study.

A Little Praise

The book *The Art of Neighboring* does raise our awareness that sometimes our neighborhoods have fallen into miscommunication, mostly driven by the proliferation of the Internet Age and increased consumerism. We are radically prodded from all an-

gles to buy, buy, buy, and this has taken root in many of our lives, Christian or otherwise. With this focus on consumerism, personal entertainment has become the end-all so as a society, more of us are driven to either work harder or enjoy the entertainment we have worked so hard to attain. In addition, we have become more wary of our world. Even in the community that spawned *The Art of Neighboring*, the few years prior lay the horrible echos of Columbine, the years of the undertaking lay the mass shooting in Aurora, CO, and shortly after, the brutal kidnapping and murder of a small child in Westminster; all three of these events were national news stories played out in the Denver metro region. Our world has become more cautious and it is a reality that kids more often play inside rather than outside for their personal safety. This book does attempt to break down some of these barriers to help people living in smaller communities become friends.

Of course I will also point out the obvious objection many would have to say to a book making light of people merely trying to make better neighborhoods: What is so wrong with learning how to better your block? This point I am not against in principle. We should know our neighbors, help them when they need help, serve them when they need served. Any Christian knows this and actually does this where possible, because the people on the block are certainly included in the people Jesus suggested would count as our neighbor. That not-with-standing, however, this book twists and wrings scripture to make a point that begins to exclude forms of service or ministry that lay outside one's own neighborhood. I would even argue the authors suggest that a person who is not making their neighborhood the first mission in their life is not obeying God.

The Art of Neighboring is not a simple text that could be given to a person who merely wants to build better neighborhood connections, but instead it is founded on a series of misinterpreted Bible verses, emotional arguments, and guilt-trip-laden statements to make the reader believe a reality that is not presented in the Bible. While my initial thoughts spanned over twenty pages of issues I have observed in the book, what is presented here is a reduced apologetic focusing on the specific challenges present in *The Art of Neighboring* as well as a correction of the passages of scripture the book uses to guilt us into believing our first ministry should always be in our neighborhood.

Challenges to a Pluralistic Time

Before we delve deeply into the theological issues with *The Art of Neighboring* I want to discuss the problems with the book in our modern world. The book does raise the issue many times of people with 'thick accents' in ways I can only guess as to the authors intentions. To me, it sounds as though the authors are conveying some form of prejudice in their comments, but I doubt that was the intention. More likely, and consistent with the writing style of the book, they were attempting to place the reader into the situation to make the reader themselves question their own prejudices. How do we really act when we meet a neighbor from a different culture? But the most curious thing I find about how this book could never work universally is the neighbor situation I presently reside among. I live in a community that has four families I know of whom share my language. Most of the block does not speak what I do, and I do

not speak what they do. The causal wave and smile is all we will ever be able to achieve unless one or both of us stop everything we do and endeavor to study one another's language. But that is just the Russian family, who by the way is very active in the local Russian church. But the people upstairs from them do not speak Russian or English. They speak Spanish, and again, neither of us have any inroad to learning the languages of the others. This does not count the numerous other cultures represented in my neighborhood complex in our highly pluralistic town.

Taken together, we have extreme barriers to becoming the types of neighbors this book suggests everyone should become, but it is not really an endeavor we should seek to do. The Russians have Russian friends in the complex and they keep together, the Spanish have the Spanish, and the English have the English. Neither of us are prejudicial to any others, but our reality is friendly smiles and waves is the best we will ever achieve in neighborly relations.

The point is, as many more people from a variety of cultures come together in society, we will start to see culturally fragmented neighborhoods by either language or cultural reasons. These people likely have friends from their own cultures, attend their own churches dedicated to their own language leaving them to want a quiet life on the block without getting too involved. The constant barrage of requests to attend a block party could actually do damage to their opinion of the neighbors. These are realities of life in twenty-first century Western cultures. Obviously I am not opposed to attempting inroads, but *The Art of Neighboring* seems to suggest the mere organization of a block party will break down the barriers and cause neighborly unity, bringing people to Jesus in droves.

Like many other church programs, however, when that does not happen in neighborhoods attempting this approach, the people will get discouraged and determine the church is really powerless.

Defining Missions

Like other 'Christian' books attempting to convince the readers to pick up it's mission, it is extremely short sighted to define the calling God may give to each of us. This book even runs contrary to many of the books in it's own bibliography! To explain, the authors of *The Art of Neighboring* try time and again to suggest our very first calling should be creating block parties to usher in some kind of community connection leading to opportunities to talk to our neighbors about Jesus. This is the opposite intention of the last recommended book in chapter two, *Radical*, by David Platt. In *Radical*, Platt tries to make the argument that we should all give away everything we have and go serve missions somewhere else. He suggests believers who do not forsake everything in their life for world missions are not obeying God. So taking these two books together, which is it? To throw block parties, get close to the neighbors, and tell them about Jesus, or become the neighbor that is never home because you sold everything and are now traveling on constant mission trips to tell people 'out there' about Jesus? The point is any book attempting to define our specific mission is blind to two realities of genuine Christian faith. First, we are a body of Christ with different purposes to fulfill. Some of us are supposed to be missionaries in our own neighborhoods and some of us should be missionaries overseas,

whether that means long term, residence-based mission work or a series of short-term missions. Additionally, some of us are merely called to raise Godly children, serve the local church in a variety of capacities (1 Timothy 3:1), or maybe something else totally outside our local congregation (Ephesians 2:10). Secondly, God should be the one giving us the calling for our life, not a book, and not our church. Our desire should be to seek God through prayer and the scriptures and ask Him how we should serve. To this point, the authors have become guilty of the same silliness we begin seeing in most of western societies: the desire to push all people to do and be the same thing. Such a cause is dangerous and it denies the specific calling God makes to His people.

Next, I suggest these authors are presenting a dangerous precedent for the church. While the parody section of this book makes lite of the Crusades in getting congregants to follow the churches mission, I think it is dangerous ground when the church starts pushing it's parsons to follow a specific plan, program, or mission. Informing or offering is one thing, but *The Art of Neighboring* was ultimately targeted to church leaders as a means to motivate church members to a specific plan. The problem is the church is not supposed to direct our missions, it is supposed to build up the believers. We should be the dedicated followers of Jesus who go to church to get away from the world, learn about God, worship Him, and be taught Biblical truth to apply in the mission work God has defined as our specific calling. Contrary to that, *The Art of Neighboring* has no mention about how to build up the people, but instead time and again focuses on throwing parties and then giving fantastical stories about when people start meeting neighbors, life goes great, and we are back to the false teaching that following Jesus will make everything OK for us in the end. The church should never define the mission work of the people, nor should she be giving false hopes about how following a carefully decided plan will make all things go well (James 4:13-16). They should be building up Biblical truth in the congregation, and for certain, offering some advice on types of missions they could do, but running a church through a program such as this book presents is dangerous at best because it tries to pigeonhole the congregation into a single goal which can confuse the specific calling God may give the individuals.

Emotional Manipulation

Neil Postman observes in his book *The Disappearance of Childhood* that emotional manipulation is a means to sell products to consumers:

> It is not facts that are offered to consumers, but idols, to which both adults and children can attach themselves with equal devotion and without the burden of logic or verification[4].

As the church begins to adopt strategies from business, we start to see the same emotional pressure applied toward church programs. This is faulty because emotional pressure can throw us off our God-given direction. The Christian life is not driven by emotional feelings. An examination of John 4:1-26 will highlight what our worship should be. In this exchange with the Samaritan woman at the well, Jesus declares we are to worship in Spirit and in Truth. While the Spirit does include some emotional response, it is more a conscience response.

The Truth component is to know the Word. But contrary to this, many church services are starting to rely on emotional arguments to move their congregants into the plan and mission of the church. The church, however, was supposed to build up the believers so they were equipped to pursue their own missions, not let the whim of the church leadership define how we should be spending our time or defining our goals. The scriptural teachings on spiritual gifts exemplifies our needs to focus on the areas God calls us to serve (Ephesians 4:11-16). But contrary to this, *The Art of Neighboring* relies more on emotional arguments than scriptural arguments, driving the readers into guilt if they do not do the things outlined in the book.

In the first chapter, the authors painstakingly appeal to our need to be a good neighbor, but instead of asking the question the teacher of the law asked of Jesus, "who is my neighbor", they instead use the statement of a local mayor to define our neighbor, "The majority of the issues that our community is facing would be eliminated or drastically reduced if *we could just figure out a way to become a community of great neighbors* [italics theirs].[5]" This quote begins a series of quotations designed to make the reader uncomfortable. For brevity, here is one of those quotes, "The ensuing discussion [with the local mayor] revealed a laundry list of social problems similar to what many cities face: at-risk kids, areas with dilapidated housing, child hunger, drug and alcohol abuse, loneliness, elderly shut-ins with no one to look in on them.[6]"

A few chapters later we find the authors talking about time barriers and we get some good secular advice about time, asking yourself what is important, and questioning the amount of time we spend in different places. All this is perfectly fine, but then we find this exact quote: "Then we suggest you prioritize the thing that Jesus says is most important – Your neighbors.[7]" I will also point out that chapter two completely twisted the parable of the Good Samaritan to define *neighbor* exclusively as the people in the houses closest to your home, but we will discuss this in more detail below. The final implication here is if we do not spend our time planning block parties and talking to the literal neighbors we are actually disobeying Jesus.

The fourth chapter about fear is nearly entirely emotional appeals. As the authors have done in prior chapters they focus on a lot of emotional statements like "Maybe there are kids in your neighborhood who are about the same age as yours. But you know their parents don't have the same values as you do, and you feel a bit uneasy every time your kids ask to go over there and play.[8]" After several such statements they conclude that you need to embrace the tension and "remember the words of Jesus [to love your literal neighbors.][9]"

The general trend of this book is to throw out arguments, sometimes from the Bible and sometimes from society and then pass along what I call Jesus Guilt Trips. Here are two more direct quotes with some context added.

Jesus Attends Parties

After talking about how Jesus often attended parties the authors talk about the gathering at Levi's house after Jesus called him to be a disciple. We see these quotes about this party:

"Levi throws this party, Jesus is more than happy to attend. After all, Levi is creating an environment where the people he knows can interact with Jesus and his new friends.[10]"

Somehow this is turned into these concluding remarks on this section:

"Let's make this personal. When we participate in block parties, we are being like Jesus.[11]"

Obeying Jesus is to Throw a Block Party

We all know the struggles an introvert has with speaking to people, but the final chapter is a summary and wrap up of the book where once again the authors attempt to fit us into a shell they created for us:

"Maybe you've tried in the past to be a good neighbor, and it hasn't gone according to plan. Not everyone is a naturally social person. You're just as content staying home as you are reaching out to others.[12]"

This is a classic introvert – such a person probably already has a full life and if they are in tune with God they are probably involved with a ministry that fits their personality. But these authors are just not content with that, "At the same time," they continue, "you want to obey Jesus and follow him wholeheartedly. You believe in the power of the Great Commandment, and you want to neighbor well.[13]" The implication here is if you are not out meeting the neighbors and planning a block party you are outside the will of God. This is dangerous to pursue.

Twisted Scripture

All the points above are merely side notes to me. The true test to any book, sermon, or teaching is how well the author wields the Sword of the Spirit. A callous handling of the Bible or twisting passages to fit a narrative are warning signs. Scripture should be handled honestly and interpreted with integrity. The Bible does not mean whatever we want it to mean as some teachers have suggested. To that end, *The Art of Neighboring* generally wields Bible with same grace a five year old handles a firearm. Several passages are misquoted or quoted out of context. While each chapter seems to have an obligatory single verse or section of the Bible, often times the authors chose scriptures that did not make sense. In many places their point could be perfectly validated using different passages in context. In other places, they are clearly stretching or making arguments from the Bible that not only are absent from the text, but lacking any Biblical support. Taken together, I believe this book is a dangerous read and the misquotations of the Bible do not justify the end-game of being a better neighbor. This section will only focus on correcting scriptures the authors have mis-quoted. First I will address the author's attempts at redefining the Great Commandment, then we will look at the other misquotations in order of appearance in the book.

What is the Great Commandment?

The authors of this book do an evil deed while attempting to redefine what they call throughout their book The Great Commandment. Some scriptural shenanigans are employed to make the point stick, then they repeat their desired end over

and over like a bad commercial attempting to break down our senses. This is critical, so we will take the time to delineate the matter, for which we need to look at all three passages in the synoptic Gospels:

> Matthew 22:37-39 - Jesus replied: "'Love the Lord your God with all your heart and with all your soul and with all your mind.' This is the first and greatest commandment. And the second is like it: 'Love your neighbor as yourself.'

> Mark 12:29-31 - "The most important one," answered Jesus, "is this: 'Hear, O Israel: The Lord our God, the Lord is one. Love the Lord your God with all your heart and with all your soul and with all your mind and with all your strength.'The second is this: 'Love your neighbor as yourself.' There is no commandment greater than these."

> Luke 10:27 - He answered, "'Love the Lord your God with all your heart and with all your soul and with all your strength and with all your mind'; and, 'Love your neighbor as yourself.'"

What we see here in the first two passages (Matthew and Mark), Jesus is speaking, answering a teacher of the law. In these, he differentiates the Greatest Commandment (which is quoted from Deuteronomy 6:5). The third passage in Luke, it is the teacher of the law saying that these two are together. Why the difference? It has to do with the focus of the passage. In Matthew and Mark, the authors were answering the question from the mouth of Jesus and then moving onto other topics. But in Luke, the emphasis was to turn the statement back around on the teacher of the law. In this instance, Jesus asks him what the law says, and so we get the teacher's answer in verse 27. Jesus then challenges the teacher of the law in verse 28 saying to "go and live likewise". But in verse 29, the teacher asks the one question this first chapter of *The Art of Neighboring* should be asking, but does not: *Who is my neighbor?*

I will note the authors never quote directly from Matthew or Mark, but only from Luke. The challenge is, however, the book does absolutely nothing to direct the reader to the first and greatest commandment according to Jesus: to love the Lord your God. In every context from the first mention of The Great Commandment to the last, the heart and God-centered focus of the verse is totally ignored, and the authors focus exclusively on loving our literal neighbor, usurping the love for the neighbor over the love for God, thus effectively placing the relationship with the neighbor as an idol over God!

The Great Commandment is to love the Lord your God with all your heart, all your mind, all your soul, and all your strength. While loving your neighbor is certainly important, it has become the primary focus in this book and the authors fail to quote from the passages to clarify that point and only focus on the passage in Luke to make it sound as if Jesus brings these two together when in reality, He does not. The Luke passage is differentiated so Jesus could expand on the very question the authors fail to properly address from the start.

Who Is My Neighbor?

In the second chapter, the authors finally tackle the question, "who is my neighbor". This is funny because for all the differences among churches, including Catholic and Protestant

brands, this is one of the only parables that has never been disputed. But these authors completely ignore what has been known about this verse through the centuries and instead come to a conclusion not found in scripture, that they actually have to use outside logic to justify!

The book does correctly assert the teacher of the law is certainly looking for a loophole to justify not loving his neighbor as himself, but Jesus tells the parable of the Good Samaritan to close every conceivable loophole to not love others.

Luke 10:30-37 - In reply Jesus said: "A man was going down from Jerusalem to Jericho, when he was attacked by robbers. They stripped him of his clothes, beat him and went away, leaving him half dead. A priest happened to be going down the same road, and when he saw the man, he passed by on the other side. So too, a Levite, when he came to the place and saw him, passed by on the other side. But a Samaritan, as he traveled, came where the man was; and when he saw him, he took pity on him. He went to him and bandaged his wounds, pouring on oil and wine. Then he put the man on his own donkey, brought him to an inn and took care of him. The next day he took out two denarii and gave them to the innkeeper. 'Look after him,' he said, 'and when I return, I will reimburse you for any extra expense you may have.' "Which of these three do you think was a neighbor to the man who fell into the hands of robbers?" The expert in the law replied, "The one who had mercy on him." Jesus told him, "Go and do likewise."

The message of the parable is simply this: *Loving your neighbor as yourself means to love people you encounter wherever they happen to be when you encounter them.* This is not just the guy in the house next door, but anyone in need whom you encounter as you live your life, wherever you happen to be.

This teaching has been clearly understood in every different undertaking I have read to understand the parables. The authors conclude the section without much comment on the parable itself and then launch into a new section specifically titled, *'Who is my neighbor?'* Once the section starts they talk about neighboring beginning with flexibility and compassion, certainly both traits of the Samaritan in the parable. But we get this snippet which starts to break down Jesus's own definition of a neighbor:

> "As we read this parable two thousand years later, it's tempting to turn the story of the good Samaritan into a metaphor...If we say, 'Everyone is my neighbor,' it can become as excuse for avoiding the implications of following the Great Commandment. Our 'neighbors' become defined in the broadest of terms. They're the people across town, the people who are helped by the organizations that receive donations, the people whom the government helps. We don't have to feel guilty, we tell ourselves. After all, we can't be expected to really love everybody, can we?[14]"

The authors here have set up a straw man argument. Jesus never said our neighbor is everyone, or the people across town, or the people in the world helped by world missions. Jesus defined a neighbor specifically as the person whom we encounter when we live our life cognizant of our surroundings. To contrast this, however, the authors want to ignore the part about 'where we are' and convert that to 'where we live'. The teacher of the law wanted a loophole which Jesus closed, but the authors of *The Art of Neighboring* give us a gaping loophole: those people whom do not live on our block are excluded from being neighbors.

The text continues:

"Today as we read this parable, we go straight for loving the neighbor on the side of the road. Thus we make a metaphor of the neighbors–a metaphor that doesn't include the person who lives next door to us. If we don't take Jesus's command literally, then we turn the Great Commandment into nothing more than a metaphor. We have a metaphoric love for our metaphoric neighbors, and our communities are changed–but only metaphorically...so in addition to thinking of our neighbor metaphorically, as did the good Samaritan, we need to apply Jesus's teaching to our literal neighbors.[15]"

This be be fine and inclusive of the literal neighbor until we find this quote later in the chapter:

"Jesus says your enemy should be your neighbor. He says you should go out of your way to be the neighbor of someone who comes from a place or history of open hostility toward you or your way of life...we would define this kind of love as advanced or graduate-level love. *The reality is that most of us aren't at the graduate level; we need to start with the basics.* [italics theirs] We need to go back to kindergarten and think about our literal next door neighbors before we attempt to love everyone else on the face of the planet.[16]"

So that is how the authors took the least debated parable of all time and completely changed the definition from meeting the needs of the people presently surrounding us to loving only those people in the neighborhood. And to be sure, I have left out a lot of meat of the book, they go into way more detail than I covered here in creating the loophole the teacher of the law so desperately wanted.

What Happened in Numbers 13?

The fourth chapter is about overcoming fear of getting to know the neighbors, but the scripture they choose to use for this section is completely twisted around. We need to start in Numbers 13. Moses sends twelve spies into the land of Canaan to determine how to best take the land, but the spies come back with this report in Numbers 13:27-29:

> They gave Moses this account: "We went into the land to which you sent us, and it does flow with milk and honey! Here is its fruit. But the people who live there are powerful, and the cities are fortified and very large. We even saw descendants of Anak there. The Amalekites live in the Negev; the Hittites, Jebusites and Amorites live in the hill country; and the Canaanites live near the sea and along the Jordan."

The spies convince the Israelites not to enter the land so they end up wandering around the desert for forty years. The authors pick up with this statement:

> "A telling statement came from Rehab, a woman who lived in the land. She explained how, years earlier, things were the opposite of what the Israelites thought were true. Joshua and Caleb had been right all along. When the spies had entered the land forty years earlier, everyone in the land was afraid of them.[17]"

Right after this statement the authors quote Joshua 2:9-11:

> "I know that the LORD has given you this land and that a great fear of you has fallen on us, so that all who live in this country are melting in fear because of you. We have heard how the LORD

dried up the water of the Red Sea for you when you came out of Egypt, and what you did to Sihon and Og, the two kings of the Amorites east of the Jordan, whom you completely destroyed. When we heard of it, our hearts melted in fear and everyone's courage failed because of you, for the LORD your God is God in heaven above and on the earth below.

The authors continue immediately after this quote:

"The Israelites' perception had been wrong all along. They had always feared their neighbors, perceiving them as giants. But in truth their neighbors feared the Israelites because of their God.[18]"

The Art of Neighboring is trying to use this part of Scripture in conjunction with the previous paraphrase to say that, according to Rehab, the people of Canaan were always afraid of the Israelites. This might pass the gaze of a Biblically uninformed audience, but I see multiple problems:

1. There is no evidence Rehab was talking about fear of the Israelites prior to meeting the two spies Joshua sent, in fact, it is more likely she is talking about the present situation, not the past, because it was known the Israelite army was camped directly across the Jordon.

2. There is no evidence the spies were seen or the people knew they were there or why (i.e. the objective of a spy is to be secret about his mission).

3. The defeat of Sihon and Og happened AFTER the twelve spies returned. Rehab would not have been afraid of the Israelites for the defeat of Sihon and Og while the twelve spies looked at the land (Og and Si-

hon were in Numbers 21 and much later in Chrono-logical history).

4. The spies sent by Moses came from Northern Paran (Numbers 13:26) but the ones from Joshua came from Shittim (Joshua 2:1), over 100 miles away in a completely different direction.

The authors want to convey that the people all gathered outside Jericho twice while the story was used to show how fear prevented the people from interacting with their neighbors...in this case, to kill them, not to have a fish fry. Nevertheless, the point of this discussion is "when we are following God into our neighborhoods, we have nothing to fear. And often it's our neighbors that need to be rescued from their fear.[19]"

The callous treatment of the scriptures in twisting this situation leads me to believe that either these pastors are totally ignorant of the Bible, or they are ignoring it to make their point. I do not know which is worse at this juncture.

Give to Get

Some online reviewers of *The Art of Neighboring* hated the message in chapter six which seemed to get pretty close to a health and wealth gospel at times. I can say I do not see that specific teaching in this book, but I can understand how some may arrive at that conclusion. The authors say, "God uses the small things that we bring him and multiplies them into a miracle in someone else's life.[20]"

The only passage of scripture in this chapter is John 6:1-13 when a small boy gives his fish and loaves to Jesus who

then performs a miracle. The most important section is verses 8-13:

> Another of his disciples, Andrew, Simon Peter's brother, spoke up, "Here is a boy with five small barley loaves and two small fish, but how far will they go among so many?" Jesus said, "Have the people sit down." There was plenty of grass in that place, and they sat down (about five thousand men were there). Jesus then took the loaves, gave thanks, and distributed to those who were seated as much as they wanted. He did the same with the fish. When they had all had enough to eat, he said to his disciples, "Gather the pieces that are left over. Let nothing be wasted." So they gathered them and filled twelve baskets with the pieces of the five barley loaves left over by those who had eaten.

This section of scripture is one of the most famous miracles Jesus performed, but the authors turn this into a lesson on what can happen in our lives if we give:

> "When you give what you have, Jesus will give you more to give. Even if what you have isn't enough to solve the whole problem, just do what you can in the moment-give it anyway. Trust that God will fill you up with enough to supply the need that's right in front of you, and assume he will do it again for the next need as well. If you don't give, you don't get a chance to see God do a miracle.[21]"

This sets a dangerous precedent all too often observed in the health and wealth community, so it merits discussion. First, we do need to give, and we need to give sacrificially, but if we give beyond our ability we can move into the field of putting God to the test, and that is also something we are commanded not to do. Secondly, if we are putting God to the test by giving away all our resources we also fail at another task: being a good steward. We should first see that our our needs are met; only after we should start to give sacrificially. That means we are not giving beyond our ability to place us in debt or miss payments, but we are giving enough to crimp our extra lifestyle. Such balance is completely missing from this section of the book.

Being Kind to Mary's Psyche

In the chapter on receiving, the authors dropped several balls to reference scriptures that are actually about receiving, but they focus on a section of scripture they mention and summarize, but curiously they do not even give us the verses. The section is Luke 7:36-50:

> When one of the Pharisees invited Jesus to have dinner with him, he went to the Pharisee's house and reclined at the table. A woman in that town who lived a sinful life learned that Jesus was eating at the Pharisee's house, so she came there with an alabaster jar of perfume. As she stood behind him at his feet weeping, she began to wet his feet with her tears. Then she wiped them with her hair, kissed them and poured perfume on them. When the Pharisee who had invited him saw this, he said to himself, "If this man were a prophet, he would know who is touching him and what kind of woman she is—that she is a sinner." Jesus answered him, "Simon, I have something to tell you." "Tell me, teacher," he said. "Two people owed money to a certain moneylender. One owed him five hundred denarii, and the other fifty. Neither of them had the money to pay him back, so he forgave the debts of both. Now which of them will love him more?" Simon replied, "I suppose the one who had the bigger debt forgiven."

"You have judged correctly," Jesus said. Then he turned toward the woman and said to Simon, "Do you see this woman? I came into your house. You did not give me any water for my feet, but she wet my feet with her tears and wiped them with her hair. You did not give me a kiss, but this woman, from the time I entered, has not stopped kissing my feet. You did not put oil on my head, but she has poured perfume on my feet. Therefore, I tell you, her many sins have been forgiven—as her great love has shown. But whoever has been forgiven little loves little." Then Jesus said to her, "Your sins are forgiven." The other guests began to say among themselves, "Who is this who even forgives sins?" Jesus said to the woman, "Your faith has saved you; go in peace."

You can see this powerful exchange is about forgiveness and how this woman was radically praising Jesus for the vast forgiveness extended to her, for Simon was right, this woman was a wretched and vile sinner before her own encounter with Jesus Christ. Rather than understanding the purpose of this exchange, *The Art of Neighboring* says this:

"She poured the perfume on Jesus in the middle of the party, perhaps making her and Jesus feeling very vulnerable and even in danger, since there were important religious men in attendance. If Jesus had rejected her offering, it would have crushed her. But he didn't. He actually went so far as to defend her...I doubt that Jesus was in great need of a foot washing and a special perfume treatment...he received it willingly because he knew that his willingness to receive this gift meant everything to her. It meant she could have dignity in her worship and that her gift counted...Jesus chose to make himself vulnerable. The one who came to give everything for us was also willing to receive from us.[22]"

This is truly twisting another very clear parable and passage into something that fits the narrative of the chapter. This is not a feel-good moment for this woman, and Jesus was not exactly taking the gift like we take the pie from the gross neighbor to toss away once our door is closed. To add further discussion, Jesus was not making himself vulnerable. To the contrary, he used this moment to correct the self-righteous indignation of the of the pharisees dining with Him.

Person of Peace

Another great fabrication to fit the narrative comes in chapter 10 on focusing. While the authors start out well quoting some scripture in proper context, we get to this point:

> "Jesus instructed them to find a certain type of person in every city they entered-a person of peace (Luke 10:5-6)...The term *person of peace* [italics theirs] refers to someone hospitable to becoming a friend...This allowed the disciples an opportunity to form deep friendships with those who were gifted at relationships themselves. Not only did they connect with the host of each house, but undoubtedly they were also introduced to the host's entire network of friends. If a person of peace was someone skilled at being hospitable, then logically they were people who would have very large networks. By directing his disciples to look for the person of peace, Jesus directed them toward those in each city who were the best neighbors.[23]"

That is a total misinterpretation of *person of peace*. This person is one whom God had sovereignly ordained to receive the message of the Gospel. This is why in the armor of God section in Ephesians, the gospel is specially called the *Gospel*

of Peace (Ephesians 6:15). The person Jesus sends out the disciples to find are people who are prepared and ready to receive the gospel. Of course, *The Art of Neighboring* is not fundamentally about Jesus or even Christian living. It's primary focus is on becoming a friend to the neighborhood, so this passage had to be castrated of it's true meaning, which is about discipleship; a lost art in the Western church. We want to get people to emotionally respond to a fire and brimstone message so they say a little prayer and then we celebrate the numbers of people who raised their hands, but then we never teach them about the Bible or their new faith. In short, they have never counted the cost of being a Christian, which Jesus commands us to do in Luke 14:25-35.

Conclusion

As the authors observed above, we are a church of immature believers, but we ought to be teachers to borrow from Hebrews. The Western Culture is actually free to own and read our Bibles. This is something most of the 'Christian' world had not experienced until only a few centuries ago, and even today many societies outright ban the ownership or study of the Bible. We in the Western cultures have access to Bibles but choose to not read them. We have access to tools, but we do not apply them, and the saddest fact of all is this book was not brought to my attention by the crazy 'over-religious' nut job, nor did I hear about it on CBN, nor spot it in a bookstore, but it was taught from, promoted, and recommended by what are considered the top churches in my town. The churches gathered together to use this book, which so horribly twisted the Bible they all profess in their doctrinal statements to hold so dear. This blew a serious hit to the confidence I placed in the churches in my local town and I pray this present parody and apologetic might rattle them out of their stupor.

While I can assert being a good neighbor to everyone we encounter (whether they are literal neighbors or strangers on the street) is a great endeavor, I care not about how great and wonderful the house is. When I go to buy a house, I examine the foundation first. If the foundation is shifty, the whole structure is in peril. Rather to explain that point further, I will let Jesus give us the final words of this book:

"Therefore everyone who hears these words of Mine and acts on them, may be compared to a wise man who built his house on the rock. And the rain fell, and the floods came, and the winds blew and slammed against that house; and *yet* it did not fall, for it had been founded on the rock. Everyone who hears these words of Mine and does not act on them, will be like a foolish man who built his house on the sand. The rain fell, and the floods came, and the winds blew and slammed against that house; and it fell—and great was its fall."

-Matthew 7:24-27

Notes

1. J. Pathak and D. Runyon, *The Art of Neighboring* (Grand Rapids: Baker Books, 2012), 50

2. H. Cloud and J. Townsend, *Boundaries* (Grand Rapids: Zondervan, 2002)

3. J. Pathak and D. Runyon, *The Art of Neighboring* (Grand Rapids: Baker Books, 2012), 140

4. N.Postman, The Disappearance of Childhood (New York: Vintage, 1994), 108

5. J. Pathak and D. Runyon, *The Art of Neighboring* (Grand Rapids: Baker Books, 2012), 19

6. Ibid, 19

7. Ibid, 54

8. Ibid, 62

9. Ibid, 64

10. Ibid, 79

11. Ibid, 80

12. Ibid, 175

13. Ibid, 175

14. Ibid, 34

15. Ibid, 35

16. Ibid, 39

17. Ibid, 65

18. Ibid, 66

19. Ibid, 66

20. Ibid, 87

21. Ibid, 89

22. Ibid, 127

23. Ibid, 147

Thomas Murosky is an author, scholar, Internet developer, blogger, and video creator. He has served in numerous capacities in churches and para-church ministries as a youth mentor and teacher. Tom's formal education lay in the life and physical sciences, earning a Bachelors Degree from Edinboro University and a Doctorate in Integrative Biosciences from Penn State University. He has taught at Bucknell University and Western Wyoming Community College before leaving academia to pursue Internet development, writing, and teaching a variety of Christian and technical topics online. You can find more about Tom at www.ourwalkinchrist.com.

This book was penned in response to the sheer number of Christian books and organizations casting aside true Biblical study and discipleship for trendy business practices and scriptural misinterpretations. While this book is intended to be a Christian comedy and parody, there is nothing funny about the way modern evangelicalism is treating the Bible. Hopefully this book will help people everywhere realize we need to stop looking for the shortcuts to God, and instead set down our digital devices, pull out that old dusty Bible, and begin true and deep study. I implore small groups to put aside video curricula and appoint a wise teacher of the Bible to teach, and for Churches to truly place the Bible above trendy business practices. Let us repent and return to God as they did in the time of Ezra, the priest.

Made in the USA
Monee, IL
02 September 2023

42032320R00090